VILLA
FOR ENGLAND
1882–2011

TREVOR FISHER

VILLA
FOR ENGLAND
1882–2011

Trevor Fisher would like to thank the following for help with this book.

At **Aston Villa**, CEO Paul Faulkner, Lee Preece, Nadine Lees, John Lerwill, Brian Doogan, Rob Bishop, and Frank Holt. **Former Players Association**, Neil Rioch, Karl Court. **Football Association**, David Barber. **National Football Museum** Peter Holmes. **Ex-Players**, Brian Little, David Platt, Nigel Spink, Gordon Cowans. **For the use of the Tommy Thompson Cartoon**, Bob Bond. **For the use of pictures,** Simon Goodyear, Mike Tilt, Roy Peters, Jon Farrelly. **For permission to quote from copyright work**, Leon Hickman, Simon Goodyear, David Platt.

Special thanks to Brian Homer for pictures and for sharing the Villa journey.

First published in Great Britain in 2011 by The Derby Books Publishing Company Limited, 3 The Parker Centre, Derby, DE21 4SZ.

This paperback edition published in Great Britain in 2013 by DB Publishing, an imprint of JMD Media Ltd

© Trevor Fisher, 2011

ISBN 978-1-78091-378-0

Printed and bound in the UK by Copytech (UK) Ltd Peterborough

Contents

Introduction 7

The Early Years 1882–1939 7
The Wilderness Years 1946–81 20
The International Challenge 1981–2011 23

Pantheon Players 32

ATHERSMITH, Charlie 32
COWANS, Gordon Sidney 35
HARDY, Samuel 44
HITCHENS, Gerry 49
PLATT, David 59
WALKER, Billy 67

Villa Internationals 74

To 27 June 2010 – England's exit from the 2010 World Cup.

Player		First	Last	Caps At Villa	Caps Total	Page
Agbonlahor	Gabriel	19 November 2008		3		74
Allen	Albert	7 April 1888	7 April 1888	1	1	77
Athersmith	Charlie	5 March 1892	7 April 1900	12	2	32
Bache	Joseph	2 March 1903	1 April 1911	7	7	79
Barrett	Earl	3 June 1991	19 June 1993	2	3	81
Barry	Gareth	31 May 2000		29		83
Barson	Frank	15 March 1920	15 March 1920	1	1	84
Bent	Darren*	1 March 2006		1	8	86
Beresford	Joseph	16 May 1934	16 May 1934	1	1	89
Blackburn	George	17 May 1924	17 May 1924	1	1	90
Brawn	William	29 February 1904	12 March 1904	2	2	91
Broome	Frank	14 May 1938	24 May 1939	7	7	92
Brown	Arthur A.	18 February 1882	13 March 1882	3	3	95
Brown	George	20 October 1926	16 November 1932	1	9	96
Collymore	Stan	3 June 1995	10 September 1997	1	3	97
Cowans	Gordon	23 February 1983	14 November 1990	8	10	35
Crabtree	James	16 March 1896	3 March 1902	11	14	100
Daley	Tony	13 November 1991	17 June 1992	7	7	102
Devey	John	5 March 1892	3 March 1894	2	2	104
Dorrell	Arthur	8 December 1924	24 October 1925	4	4	105
Downing	Stuart*	16 August 2006		1		106
Dublin	Dion	11 January 1998	18 November 1998	1	4	109
Ducat	Andy	12 February 1910	23 October 1920	3	6	110
Ehiogu	Ugo	23 May 1996	27 March 2002	1	4	112

				Caps		
Player		**First**	**Last**	**At Villa**	**Total**	**Page**
Gardner	Thomas	16 May 1934	18 May 1935	2	2	113
Garratty	William	2 March 1903	2 March 1903	1	1	114
George	William (Billy)	3 March 1902	3 May 1905	3	3	115
Gidman	John	30 March 1977	30 March 1977	1	1	117
Hall	Albert	12 February 1910	12 February 1910	1	1	118
Hampton	Harry	17 March 1913	4 April 1914	4	4	119
Hardy	Sam	18 March 1907	10 April 1920	7	21	44
Hendrie	Lee	18 November 1998	18 November 1998	1	1	122
Heskey	Emile	16 November 2003	27 June 2010	17	62	123
Hitchens	Gerry	19 May 1961	10 June 1962	3	7	49
Hodge	Steve	6 June 1986	1 May 1991	11	24	127
Hodgetts	Denis	4 February 1888	3 March 1894	6	6	129
Houghton	Eric	20 October 1930	1 December 1932	7	7	130
James	David	23 March 1997	27 June 2010	3	53	134
Kirton	William	22 October 1921	22 October 1921	1	1	135
Leake	Alexander	12 March 1904	1 April 1905	5	5	136
Little	Brian	21 May 1975	21 May 1975	1	1	137
Lowe	Eddie	3 May 1947	25 May 1947	3	3	140
Merson	Paul	11 September 1991	18 November 1998	1	21	142
Milner	James	12 August 2009		11		144
Morley	Tony	18 November 1981	17 November 1982	6	6	146
Mort	Thomas	3 March 1924	17 April 1926	3	3	149
Moss	Frank (Snr)	22 October 1921	19 April 1924	5	5	150
Olney	Ben	17 May 1928	19 May 1928	2	2	151
Platt	David	15 November 1989	26 June 1996	22	62	59
Reynolds	John	2 April 1892	3 April 1897	5	8	153
Richardson	Kevin	17 May 1994	17 May 1994	1	1	155
Smart	Tommy	9 April 1921	20 November 1929	5	5	156
Smith	Steve	8 April 1895	8 April 1895	1	1	158
Southgate	Gareth	18 June 1996	31 March 2004	42	57	159
Spencer	Howard	29 March 1897	1 April 1905	6	6	161
Spink	Nigel	19 June 1983	19 June 1983	1	1	163
Starling	Ronnie	1 April 1933	17 April 1937	1	2	165
Tate	Joe	14 May 1931	15 November 1932	3	3	166
Thompson	Thomas	20 October 1951	6 April 1957	1	2	168
Vassell	Darius	13 February 2002	24 June 2004	22	22	169
Vaughton	Howard	18 February 1882	17 March 1884	5	5	170
Walker	Billy	23 October 1920	7 December 1932	18	18	67
Wallace	Charles	17 March 1913	10 April 1920	3	3	172
Waring	Pongo	14 May 1931	9 April 1932	5	5	175
Warnock	Stephen*	1 June 2008		1		178
Whateley	Oliver	24 February 1883	10 March 1883	2	2	180
Wheldon	George 'Fred'	20 February 1897	2 April 1898	4	4	182
Wilkes	Albert	18 March 1901	3 May 1902	5	5	183
Withe	Peter	12 May 1981	14 November 1984	11	11	184
York	Richard	8 April 1922	19 April 1926	2	2	188
Young	Ashley*	31 August 2007		14		189

*up to and including 7 February 2011

Note: Players must be capped while playing for the Villa to count. Caps awarded before or after appearing for Villa do not count. Paul Merson only got one cap while at Villa but counts. Mark Walters won his caps after leaving so does not count. First and last caps and of caps won are for total career. If still playing for England, no final total given.

Bibliography   192

Introduction

The Early Years 1882–1939

The background: internationals before the rule book

Aston Villa's international record starts in 1882, when Howard Vaughton and Arthur (AA) Brown were picked to play for England against Ireland. The international scene in 1882 was very different to the picture today. There was no international competition, and no thought of playing outside the UK. Only the four home countries played each other and then only in friendlies. The Ireland match was the first international between the two countries.

The Home Countries were only just setting themselves up. A decade earlier the first official international match in history had taken place when England played Scotland in Glasgow. This match in 1872 actually took place before the Scottish FA was set up, in 1873, but the formation of the Scottish Association led to the Welsh and Irish forming their own associations

It was a pretty chaotic birth to a world sport. No other countries had got anyway near forming enough clubs to think about national teams, and there was no internationally accepted rulebook. Each country had its own rules and when England traveled to away matches they played under the local rules – so Vaughton and Brown would have played under Irish rules. This was not a sensible way to organise matches, and on 6 December 1882 the English Football Association (FA) persuaded the other three Home Countries at a meeting in Manchester to agree one rule book and an international board to decide on future changes. The way was open for international soccer competitions to begin.

The early years of Villa internationals

The selection of the two Villa players was a sign of the mushroom growth of the sport in the industrial towns of England. Villa were formed as recently as 1874 and like most clubs at that time were just a group of friends playing to keep fit in the winter. The Villa team were men from a Weslyan chapel in Lozells, who hired a pitch to play on at the Aston Lower Grounds. Hundreds of teams were forming in the same way, and most fell by the wayside in the next 20 years. But the Villa committee were talented people, and attracted talented players.

By 1880, when Villa won their first trophy, the Birmingham Senior Cup, the reputation of the club attracted attention outside the Second City. Their best two English players were invited to travel to Belfast to play Ireland. Vaughton and Brown scored on their debut – Vaughton's five making him the first player ever to score five in an international – and Villa were a recognised force only eight years after formation. Many other small clubs had players selected, however, and though another Villa player would be selected in the early 1880s – Oliver Whateley, an amateur player – there was no guaruntee that Villa would survive. The growth of Villa was due to clever planning by the committee, notably its first captain and then secretary, a Scot working in Birmingham, George Ramsay.

In 1878, Ramsay found a pitch in Perry Barr which could be fenced off to allow paid admission. This was crucial in putting the club on a sound financial basis. Villa supported professionalism and a League structure and these required increased revenue. The second key move was the signing of a new and influential captain. When Archie Hunter came to Birmingham to work he was directed to Villa where Ramsay who was also an exiled Scot saw his talent and signed him up, the first of the great Villa players.

The Perry Barr ground started the club gaining the funds vital if professionalism was legalised. Villa were one of the clubs pushing for the legalisation of professionalism, but the assumption of the FA was that the game would remain largely amateur. Indeed, two of Villa's first three internationals, Vaughton and Oliver Whateley, were amateurs. Like Vaughton and Brown, both born in Aston, Whateley was a local man but working as an artist and designer. Coming from a wealthy background, he had no problem in playing for England when called up for two games in 1883. But workers could not take time off work and lose money, which perhaps explains why for the next five years no Villa man was selected for England.

The FA agreed to payment for players in 1885. Villa would have a few amateurs for several decades, but on the whole the club was now largely professional. With the Scots contingent led by George Ramsay introducing Scots players and methods into the Villa style, Villa were pioneers. The International record of England in the first few years showed that, while England could normally beat Wales and Ireland easily, the Scots were equally better than England. This was because they played a passing game, pioneered by Queens Park (Glasgow), the amateur club, not to be confused with QPR in London. They entered the FA Cup till the mid-1880s when the Scots FA, alarmed by the number of Scots players going to England to take up paid positions banned Scots clubs from the FA Cup. It did not stop the drain of players to richer English clubs. The English thought passing was unmanly and a player should dribble the ball till stopped by an opponent. The international results gave food for thought.

Villa were among the first English clubs to adopt the Scottish style, and it was this which led to their golden age from 1887. Ramsay, as captain and then from 1884 secretary and effectively manager, could not fail to notice that the Scots were more successful than the English. In 1882, Ramsay invited Queens Park down from Glasgow to study the style of the famous amateur club at first hand. Queens Park came down with their formation featuring two full-backs – virtually unknown in England, where attack was the key and six forwards were employed – and beat Villa 4–1. Villa then adopted two full-backs and laid the foundations of the W formation – two full-backs, three half-backs and five forwards – which ruled till another Ramsay, the English manager Alf, invented the wingless wonder formation and won the World Cup in 1966.

George Ramsay brought the Scottish style into Villa's play, developing the passing game involving players playing the ball out of defence not simply kicking it to the forwards. This was the key to Villa's first successful bid for a national trophy, the campaign which led to Villa winning the FA Cup for the first time in April 1887. The selectors could no longer ignore Villa players, and sought the new players coming through at Perry Barr. Villa had a fourth player picked for the England side in February 1888, the forward Denis Hodgetts, who scored in a 5–1 home victory. Hodgetts was picked a second time in March against Ireland, along with Albert Allen who scored a hat-trick in another 5–1 victory. No Villa player was then picked for four years, whether because their style was not for England or because they wanted to concentrate on playing for the Villa is not known. But from 1892 for a dozen years Villa players were in demand

The Golden Age of Aston Villa; reputation gained 1890–99

Villa were building a new style of operation, aided by the formation of the Football League in 1888 – started by Villa's forward-looking Scots secretary, William McGregor. With only the FA Cup to rely on, the system of friendlies had been too unreliable to keep a paid squad of players going – matches were often called off on the morning of the games, and the flow of cash was uncertain. A League structure provided regular finance.

The man who made the Football League. William McGregor invented regular fixtures and transformed world football.

Villa had a slow start. Preston North End, Everton and Sunderland dominated for the first five seasons. Villa regrouped and from 1893–94 when they won the League became the outstanding club in England. In the Cup they lost to Albion in 1892 but won a second trophy in 1895 and again in 1897. The League was even better with Championships in 1896, 1897, 1899 and 1900, achieving the Cup double in 1897 on the club's fourth Cup Final appearance.

The 1892 Cup defeat was the result which triggered the famous Barwick St meeting, which appointed Frederick Rinder to be the financial secretary of the club. Rinder introduced turnstiles at Wellington Road in 1895 to boost takings. Increased finance co-incided with Villa's best-ever period and the move back to Aston. Villa were able to pay the more pricey lease of the old Lower Grounds site and help build the biggest and best purpose built stadium in the country – opened in time for Villa to stage an international in 1899. A dozen years later, Villa had the money to buy the ground and own its own home.

Success on and off the pitch fed through into recognition at international level. Hodgetts was recalled in the spring of 1892, gaining his fourth cap alongside William (Charlie) Athersmith and John Devey, against Ireland. The others did not appear for the game against Scotland in April – suprisingly Athersmith would not be capped again till 1897 – but in the spring of 1894 Hodgetts won his sixth and last cap, Devey his second and to general astonishment his last, and John Reynolds won his first cap as a Villa player, but his fourth in total – his first three as a West Brom player. The fact that Villa could attract the Albion's best player showed that in the local rivalry between Villa and Albion, the balance was slowly swinging toward the Villa.

The Villa only had one player in the April 1894 game against Scotland, Reynolds scoring the equaliser in his fifth game. On 6 April 1895 in the home fixture against the Scots Reynolds won his sixth cap alongside Stephen Smith of the Villa, scoring the winning goal in a 3–0 victory. Despite this, he was never capped again. With Villa having won their first League Championship the previous year (1894), it is suprising they only had two players in the England team. The situation was even more puzzling in 1896, for only James Crabtree, signed from Burnley, was picked for the three internationals that year though the club was on the crest of a wave.

By the 1897 fixtures, the famous year of the Cup and League double, the club was back in favour. Athersmith was recalled for his second cap, scoring his first England goal, and starting a run of three seasons (1897, 98 and 99) in which he would be ever present, playing all three matches each year. He played alongside George Wheldon in the first match of 1897, the only other Villa player to be selected. Wheldon celebrated his first cap with a hat-trick. Suprisingly, Crabtree did not appear in 1897 or 1898. Wheldon was also missing the next two internationals in the spring of 1897. The club was too dominant to ignore, however, and for the first time since 3 March 1894 three Villa players played for England. Howard Spencer for his first cap, John Reynolds recalled for his seventh, and Athersmith for his third. Overall in the three games of 1897 four Villa players were capped – Athersmith for all three, Reynolds and Spencer for two, and Wheldon for one.

How selections were made and what role availability, injury or political wrangling played a part is impossible to establish. Athersmith was a regular, but Reynolds, Wheldon and Spencer were in and out.

But in February Athersmith played alongside Crabtree who earned his seventh cap having been recalled after two years in the wilderness. Both men now became fixtures for the season, playing in the legendary April game against the Scots, the first ever to be held at Villa Park and the fixture which allows the ground to be hailed as holding internationals in three separate centuries. This game on 8 April 1899 allowed the Villa fans to see Athersmith and Crabtree playing as internationals. No one could doubt the club was on the crest of a wave, and as England won 2–1 the fans went home happy. Perhaps they wondered why only these two merited caps from a team about to win the Championship. This historian is also puzzled.

Athersmith and Crabtree played against Wales at Cardiff Arms Park on 26 March 1900. They were joined by Howard Spencer, gaining his third cap and first since April 1897 and once again Villa provided three players. It appeared Villa were starting the third of their great decades in good shape, but in fact their two leading players were coming to the end of their careers peaking with Championship medals for a second successive Championship in 1900.

Athersmith and Crabtree gained their 12th caps on 7 April 1900 playing against Scotland at Celtic Park in a 4–1 defeat. Athersmith would never play for England again – he left Villa for Birmingham City that year and his career at the top was over. Crabtree would gain two more caps alongside Albert Wilkes, whose caps showed that the Villa machine for turning out internationals was still working. Crabtree made his 14th and last appearance for England alongside Wilkes, gaining his third cap, and William George, gaining his first, on 3 March 1902

It was the end of an era. Villa remained near the top of the tree in terms of winning honours, though they would never again be as successful as in the period 1892–1900.

The Villa after Athersmith and Crabtree: Reputation defended 1900–1909

From 1894 to 1905, a 12-year period, not a year had gone by without at least one Villa player capped for England, and usually more than one. There were individual games where no Villa players appeared, and some players vanished and then returned, even Athersmith and Crabtree. But the selectors always had to consider the Villa squad. After 1905, this was less automatic. Only Spencer of the players picked in the 1890s would appear in teams after 1900. Villa might have expected more players to be picked. Spencer was highly regarded, and became captain if selected, but his availability was sporadic. This was true of all Villa players. None emulated Crabtree and Athersmith for regular selection.

The most favoured was Joe Bache, Villa captain after Howard Spencer, who picked up Cup-winners' medals in 1905 and 1913 and a Championship medal in 1910. Bache was multi-talented, but even he could not command a regular place for England, appearing only seven times in nine years – when 27 home internationals and some friendlies were played.

Other players were even less fortunate. William George, Albert Wilkes, Billy Brawne, Alec Leake, William Garratty all had few chances to shine. With Howard Spencer gaining only seven caps in eight years, it was less easy to gain caps for England. Even Joe Bache only gained seven in nine seasons in which Villa won the League, came second twice, and won the FA Cup. Competition was becoming ever fiercer, as more clubs gained their own grounds, large fan bases and professional training grounds, Amateurs and public school boys were vanishing and professionally trained players were dominating.

The increasing number and professionalism of teams meant that the pool of talent was increasing. From 1888 to 1891 there had only been 12 professional League teams. The creation of the second division in 1892 meant there were 28 teams – 16 in Division One – and this increased to 40 in the period

1905–15, 20 in each division. The larger pool of talent meant more players could be selected, so the players selected had to be better than before. Clubs moreover could no longer rely on local talent or players from other parts of the UK arriving on their doorstep. Training, recruitment, and the conditions at a club all played an increasingly important part in getting good players on board though the maximum wage kept a level playing field between clubs. However transfer fees were key. Big fees kept rising.

When in August 1895 Villa signed James Crabtree from Burnley for £250, it was said to be an outrageous waste of money. A year later Fred Wheldon was signed from Small Heath (later Birmingham City) for £350. Then Martin Watkins from Stoke at £400 in January 1904 – Villa beat the opposition because Manchester City could not afford such an astonishing fee. The club transfer record was broke again in 1907 in signing Charlie Wallace from Crystal Palace. These experiences showed that large fees were good investments – if the right players were bought. Villa did well in the years before World War One. When the club broke the record again in signing Andy Ducat from Woolwich Arsenal in June 1912, the club's first four-figure signing at £1,000, they were again signing a winner who had already won caps for England and would go on to do so while at Villa – albeit after World War One.

By 1914 Villa was matching the growing competition in all the fields created by an expanding and developing football world. As the club celebrated 40 years of growth in 1914, it looked forward with confidence. After all, it had won the League Championship for a record sixth time in 1910. The team that won the Championship had faded, but new players replaced them. No Villa player won a cap in the two years before March 1913, but then Harry Hampton and Charlie Wallace won their first caps. Sam Hardy joined in goal from Liverpool, winning his 14th cap, and first for Villa, in February 1914. Famously, the poet Philip Larkin, looking back later at 1914 and the outbreak of the Great War, described the scene outside army recruiting offices like the 'lines standing patiently as if they were stretched outside the Oval or Villa Park'. These were the two largest sporting stadiums in the country. Villa seemed set fair to regroup after the war was over.

Back from the trenches: growing competition at home and abroad 1919–39

When football started again in 1919, while only Hardy kept his place initially,

Andy Ducat was recalled for three more caps, and astonishingly Charlie Wallace was recalled for his last cap after a gap of nine years. But these were stop gaps after the long wartime break, into which Harry Hampton and many others fell, too old to come back. But Villa appeared well set for the future. There were going to be more internationals, and so more caps to be won. The Four Home Nations turned their back on FIFA, but too many men had gone abroad in the war to ignore Europe any longer. Friendlies became common, to start with against the war time allies France and Belgium. Later Luxembourg, Sweden, Austria and even the enemy in the war, Germany, joined the list. It was informal. Some years only the old traditional Home Championship took place with the four home countries – 1920 and 1922 for example. But most years the England team could travel abroad.

But increased competition meant a higher standard of players, and less reliance on local heroes. Villa found it harder to pick winners. In 1919, for example, Villa broke their transfer record, signing Frank Barson at half-back for £2,850 from Barnsley. His talent was undeniable, and he won one cap in 1920. But Barson's aggression overstepped the mark into violence, and he was sold in 1922 to Manchester United for £5,000 as too unpredictable. In theory, he moved because he would not live in Birmingham. With more top clubs, Villa could not demand the same loyalty as before the war; players could pick and choose. But the bigger issue was that Villa was not as attractive as in its golden period.

This was not obvious for over a decade, and the 1920s promised to be good for Villa. In 1920 they won the FA Cup for the sixth time, starring a new centre-forward who almost immediately won the first of 18 caps – Billy Walker, a local lad from the Black Country. The caps kept coming. Tommy Smart, forming a formidable full-back partnership with Tommy Mort, 'Death and Glory', won five caps between 1921 and 1929. Mort won three between 1924 and 1926, and in the same year that Smart won his first cap Frank Moss won the first of his five. Although his international career lasted only three years, it peaked in 1924 with the England captaincy. Moss captained Villa and England in two memorable weekends in 1924, a sign that Villa were still a major force. But Villa had lost the Cup Final for the first time since the 1892 appearance, and as in 1892 this would be followed by trouble in the boardroom. George Blackburn won his only cap after appearing in the Cup Final shop window. In 1922 Richard York had won the first of his two caps, like Frank Moss a local lad.

TEAMS FOR TO-DAY'S MATCH—SATURDAY, APRIL 8th, 1922.

INTERNATIONAL MATCH.

SCOTLAND v. ENGLAND

Kick-off at 3 p.m.

SCOTLAND.

Right. Left.

K. CAMPBELL (1)
(Partick Thistle)

JOHN MARSHALL (2) JAMES BLAIR (3)
(Middlesbrough) *(Cardiff City)*

JNO. GILCHRIST (4) W. CRINGAN (5) NEIL M'BAIN (6)
(Celtic) *(Celtic)* *(Manchester United)*

A. ARCHIBALD (7) J. CROSBIE (8) A. WILSON (9) T. CAIRNS (10) A. L. MORTON (11)
(Rangers) *(Birmingham)* *(Middlesbrough)* *(Rangers)* *(Rangers)*

RESERVES: PETER KERR (Hibernians) and JOHN WHITE (Albion Rovers).

REFEREE: MR. T. DOUGARY (Bellshill, Scotland).
LINESMEN: MESSRS. J. F. PEARSON (Dudley) and A. G. ADAMSON (Fife).

W. H. SMITH (12) W. H. WALKER (13) W. E. RAWLINGS (14) R. KELLY (15) R. E. YORK (16)
(Huddersfield Town) *(Aston Villa)* *(Southampton)* *(Burnley)* *(Aston Villa)*

T. G. BROMILOW (19) G. WILSON, Capt. (18) F. MOSS (19)
(Liverpool) *(The Wednesday)* *(Aston Villa)*

S. J. WADSWORTH (20) T. CLAY (21)
(Huddersfield Town) *(Tottenham Hotspur)*

J. DAWSON (22)
(Burnley)

Left. Right.

RESERVES: P. BARTON (Birmingham) and J. SEED (Tottenham Hotspur).

ENGLAND.

In the event of any alteration in the above teams, a board giving particulars will be sent round the ground.

The legendary 1922 game with Scotland at Villa Park.
The formation is the classic W pattern: five forwards,
three half-backs, two full-backs and a goalkeeper.

However, the era when players like Moss and York could still emerge from the local teams in North Birmingham was coming to an end. Villa were not well organised and lacked the new innovation of a manager, still being run by a committee. In crucial areas like scouting and training the club was falling behind. Fred Rinder was a dominant chair, but he was getting older and his obsession with the ground and being a disciplinary force was not producing the goods on the playing field. In 1921 Rinder and the Committee fell out with four key players over not living in Birmingham, Sam Hardy, James Harrop – both veterans whose career was coming to an end – the difficult Frank Barson, and Clem Stephenson. Barson was a serious loss, and Clem Stephenson leaving created a hole Villa could not fill.

Stephenson was an inside-forward who won Cup medals in 1913 and 1920 and, though 31 when he fell out with the club and left for Huddersfield, was a football genius as the manager Herbert Chapman recognised. Chapman took him to Huddersfield, where he captained the side to three successive League titles, won the FA Cup in 1922 and played in the losing Final in 1928. He then managed the club from 1929, taking them to two Cup Finals.

That Stephenson in his thirties achieved his greatest triumphs after leaving not only showed Villa had missed his potential, but he was part of the Herbert Chapman revolution. Chapman was one of the all-time great managers. He won titles with Huddersfield and then Arsenal. In London he had the local tube station renamed Arsenal. Even now, Villa still have not followed Chapman's lead and got Witton Station named Villa Park. Unlike Arsenal under Chapman, Villa did not have a manager. Villa still thought a committee was good enough.

This was despite clear signs of decline. In 1924 Arthur Dorrell won the first of his four caps, partnering Billy Walker, now converted to inside-forward, on the left wing. But Billy Walker was the only established player at England level, and the team as a whole struggled. Since the start of football in 1919 after the end of World War One, Villa had never come higher than fifth.

But far worse was the financial situation. Rinder had built a fine new stand on the Trinity Road, opened in 1924 – the second to be built, and knocked down in 2000 to build the present structure. The accounts for 1925 showed the cost was twice that of the estimates, and the row saw Rinder kicked off the board and replaced as chair by Director Jack Jones. It seemed to be enough. While no Villa player was capped for two years apart from the odd selection of goalkeeper Ben Olney, a new team was being built under Jones's leadership.

There seemed no need for a new style manager. George Ramsay had finally retired in 1926 after an astonishing half century of service, and Villa advertised for a secretary-manager. The club appointed assistant secretary Billy Smith who ran team matters, and it seemed to work. Villa came third in 1929 and fourth in 1930. With an exciting new forward line, Houghton replacing Dorrell and Pongo Waring coming in as a traditional battering ram centre-forward, the stage was set for a classic confrontation with the new force in English soccer Arsenal – under Chapman, the first of the great overall managers. This would be the old style of club versus the new style.

Rising to a peak and falling from grace

The battle took place over three seasons, from 1930–31 to 1932–33. Eric Houghton won his first caps in 1930, with half-back Joe Tate and Pongo Waring joining him in the England squad in 1931. The power of Villa's forward line was immense, with Waring scoring 49 League goals in a record total of 128. But Arsenal were almost equally good with 127 goals, and had a much better defence – 59 goals conceded as against Villa's 78. Villa came second, gaining 59 points to Arsenal's 66 (two points for a win). Both sides fell back in 1931–32, Arsenal coming second to Dixie Dean's Everton and Villa fifth, but the battle resumed in 1932–33 – and Arsenal again topped the table, beating Villa into second place by 58 points to 54. Villa fans looked forward with anticipation, but it was the end of an era. Not for another 48 years would Villa come in the top two again. Arsenal would win three titles in succession. Villa had lost the battle and were heading into decline.

It was the end of an era for Billy Walker, who had been sensationally recalled for his 18th cap in 1932 to skipper England against the magnificent Austrians, but never played again for England. He then left the club in January 1933 to manage Sheffield Wednesday, and again as with Clem Stephenson the club allowed a top managerial talent to leave. He took the post of secretary-manager at the Wednesday, a club which had just finished third and which he would take to win the FA Cup in 1935. In Billy Smith Villa had a man in the key job who had never played professional football and was an administrator. Villa tried copying the Herbert Chapman formula, George Brown had been bought in 1929 for £5,000 from Huddersfield but he won only one cap with the Villa in 1932 to add to the eight he had won with the Terriers. His career wound down at Villa Park.

Villa failed to get any international recognition in 1933 or 1934 – the years Stanley Matthews and Raich Carter broke through at England level and Arsenal supplied seven players in a friendly against Italy. While Arsenal remained top of the table, Villa slipped into mid-table mediocrity. The argument for a manager was now unanswerable On 11 May 1934, after Villa had finished 13th and Arsenal topped the League, Jimmy McMullan, a former Scottish international, was made Villa's first manager.

It is unlikely he had any real power. Billy Smith never accepted he could not control the team, and once broke into a team talk and swept the tactics table onto the floor to humiliate McMullan. Pongo Waring had fierce rows with the manager. In 1934–35 Villa again finished 13th, and recorded the first financial loss save for the war years. The Gibson, Talbot and Tate half-back line – Wind, Sleet and Rain – was gone and their replacements were not good enough. In 1935–36 the defence conceded 110 goals, the only side in the division to concede more than 100, and already McMullan had given in, resigning the previous October. The board was now in charge again under Billy Smith, who with the directors and Frank Barson, the prodigal son now back coaching the reserves, spent £35,000, a record sum, in the last three months of the season as panic set in. It was too late. Villa were relegated for the first time in their history.

Heads rolled on the board, Howard Spencer resigning and Jack Jones being removed from the chair. Fred Rinder, at 79, was re-elected to the board and is credited with getting the club back in the black and making the next crucial move – a real manager was appointed, the legendary Jimmy Hogan, in the summer of 1936. Billy Smith remained secretary till after World War Two, but Hogan reorganised the training methods and recruited young players. After signing in January 1937, Ronald Starling did get a cap to add to the one he had gained while at Sheffield Wednesday. But Starling at 27 was not a force for the future and never gained another cap.

The Jimmy Hogan era can be seen as a rebuilding job which was never finished because of the war. Hogan took two years to get Villa promoted and then had only one year in Division One settling in the First Division before World War Two broke out, but his managership had one bright spot. Hogan coached Villa's lost genius – Frank Broome. Almost totally forgotten today, apart from the length of his time at the club (two months short of 12 years on the books, disrupted by wartime friendlies for other clubs), Broome was the last great player of the interwar era.

Frank Broome emerged during the promotion campaigns of 1936–38, top scoring in each of the three seasons before the war. The England selectors took note, and a week after his last match in Division two, Broome was playing for England in Berlin – in the notorious Hitler Salute match. Broome scored, and though rested in other matches made three other appearances in 1938. Overall he played in seven of the last 12 international before the war, including the last three games for England before Hitler invaded Poland and brought football to an end. And he played with legends – Eddie Hapgood, Stan Cullis, Joe Mercer, Stanley Matthews, Tommy Lawton, and Wilf Copping. Judging a player by the company he keeps, Broome was in the top drawer. Broome lost the six years of wartime service, and never recovered his place in the England side. But to gain seven caps for his country at a time when Villa were only slowly recovering from relegation shows a very high level of talent.

The 1930s are a decade of disappointment and underachievement for the Villa. But Broome showed that the well of talent was not dry, that Hogan could develop potential. But the war years ended Hogan's career. When football resumed in 1946 what would the future hold for Aston Villa?

The Wilderness Years 1946–81

The aftermath of war sees Villa fall behind

When football restarted in 1946 after the war it became clear that Villa was suffering from major problems. These would not be resolved for over 30 years. The Wilderness Years until Villa again managed to enter the top two of the League saw them virtually incapable of producing players for the English team. The record is very clear, and deeply sad. In 35 years Villa had five players who played for England – one every seven years – and won only nine caps between them, an average of less than two per player. Some Cup success did not compensate for overall mediocrity.

The record speaks for itself. Eddie Lowe won three caps with the Villa, Tommy Thompson one, breaking through at England level roughly five years apart. Then after another five years or so, Gerry Hitchens won his three Villa caps. There was then a fourteen year gap before Brian Little won his solitary cap, and two years later John Gidman won one as Villa climbed back into, and established itself in, the very top division. In 32 years Villa players won only nine caps. It was the worst period in club history, as the problems threatening in the 1930s proved after the war to be so deep rooted that they wrecked the club over a 25-year period. By 1970 Villa were in the third division.

When football resumed after six years of war, Villa had suffered less physical damage than other clubs. Old Trafford had been bombed to destruction and other grounds had physical scars. Yet Manchester United and other clubs bounced back when Football resumed to record crowds starved of entertainment. Villa drifted into mid-table mediocrity. The Home International Championships were declining in importance and would eventually be abandoned. The four-yearly cycle of World Cup qualification, followed two years later by European Championships, now dominated the scene. There were more games than ever before as friendlies became more frequent. But the other side of the coin was that with more and more games, competition for places became infinitely greater. Villa were not competing.

Within the game as a whole, the decade after the end of the war was an era of golden talent and modern management, based on the all powerful manager like Matt Busby at Manchester United and Billy Nicholson at Tottenham. Even England had appointed its first manager, after FA secretary Stanley Rous had persuaded the stuffed shirts who ran the Association to agree to the post. Walter Winterbottom took charge of a footballing treasure house. One writer comments that he 'had at his disposal a glut of talent unparalleled in the history of the English game' (*ENGLAND EXPECTS,* James Corbett, Aurum 2006, p.92). Alas, Aston Villa hardly began to feature in supplying the glut. Frank Broome never recovered his superb pre-war form and, while Alex Massie as manager tried to re-introduce high-quality football, he was hampered by board room incompetence, a dressing room sceptical of a man who went straight from playing to managing and fans too impatient to tolerate a skilful passing game. The scouting system was inadequate – it missed Duncan Edwards, greatest talent of the 1950s, who was from the Black Country where old heroes like Billy Walker had come from, and Gerry Hitchens, who was picked up from a Shropshire miners team by Kidderminster and had go to Cardiff before arriving at Villa Park. When Villa did sign talent, as with Danny Blanchflower, the player soon wanted away.

The false dawn: Massie, Martin and Mercer

The Villa had gone back to the old system of the chair and the secretary – Fred Normansell and Billy Smith – making the key decisions. In the four years he was nominally manager, Alex Massie later said, transfers were made over his head.

And the men signed by Normansell and Smith were not international quality. Worse, fans would not tolerate the skilful passing game Massie wanted with relegation an increasing threat. Route-one football was safe. But it did not develop international players. Only Eddie Lowe made the England team, gaining three caps in 1947, then Eddie and his brother, Reg, quit the club for Fulham, a division below, after Massie resigned in July 1949. Villa had fought off relegation in 1947–48 and achieved mid-table respectability the following season, but managing the Villa was too challenging with the club unattractive to top talent.

Not that the fans noticed. The lack of protest is astonishing, and the Villa fan base was showing that it had a complacent streak as massive as that of the underperforming board. At the 1950 AGM club president Sir Patrick Hannon stated members of the club were 'a body of fans working in harmony'. Or sleep walking toward disaster. The board sold its best player, Trevor Ford, for £30,000 in the close season without protest. It is a remarkable that it would be nearly 20 years before there was a fans protest – and by 1969 the club was nearly bankrupt.

The next manager, George Martin, started well, signing a football genius in Danny Blanchflower in March 1951. But Blanchflower would star for Spurs, not Villa, asking for a transfer in October 1954 when he realised the club was going nowhere. As far as England caps were concerned, the board had scored a success in signing Tommy Thompson in September 1950, and he was capped for England in October 1951, but he failed to develop and, despite scoring 76 goals in 165 first-class games, he got a transfer to Preston in June 1955, where he could play with Tom Finney, and later to Stoke, where he played with Stanley Matthews. There were no players of that quality at Villa Park.

Villa dismissed Martin in August 1953 and the club appointed their star of the 1930s, Eric Houghton, as the new manager. Despite winning the FA Cup in 1957, Houghton could not lift the club higher than sixth in the table, and in

Tommy Thompson.

November 1958, with the club sliding towards relegation, he resigned. His successor, Joe Mercer, could not stop the club being relegated but brought the club back up in 1960, started a youth policy, and polished an uncut diamond of a player – Gerry Hitchens – into an international class player. The development of Gerry Hitchens into a world-class player by Mercer and his staff should have provided the opening of a new era. But in 1961 after only a handful of caps, Hitchens left England and its maximum wage to forge a new life in Italy.

With Hitchens's departure, Villa drifted into the worst decade in its history. Mercer had a nervous breakdown and moved to Manchester City and success. He left behind a club in crisis. Relegation to Division Two had been known before. Relegation to Division Three was unprecedented, yet it happened in 1970, despite a new board taking power. After long years of recovery under Vic Crowe and Ron Saunders, Villa came back to Division One in 1975, with a nucleus of excellent young players. Docherty and Crowe had both supported a new youth policy, returning to the old Villa tradition of developing their own players. In 1972 Villa won the FA Youth Cup for the first time. Several of this team made careers in the First Division, but only Brian Little and John Gidman were capped for England, and then they could only win one cap each. In truth, a club which was still recovering and had not made any real impact on the First Division and, with limited experience in Europe, was not going to gain much international status. But in 1981 under Ron Saunders, Villa finally climbed back into the top two after 48 years, winning the League title for the first time since 1910. The years in the wilderness were finally over.

The International Challenge 1981–2011

The success of the Saunders's players –Withe, Morley, Cowans

When Aston Villa won the Championship in 1981, it was a triumph not trumpeted widely by the media. Opinion formers favoured the Tractor Boys of Ipswich Town, lovable to outsiders and managed by the personable Bobby Robson. Ipswich were unlikely to threaten the darlings of the media in London and the North, whereas Aston Villa were the one Midlands club who could do just that. Nevertheless, Villa had won on merit with a four point gap over their rivals. It was the last season when two points were awarded for a win. Had the system of three points for a win been in place, Villa would have got 86 points in 1981 and Ipswich 79, a seven-point gap. In 1982 Liverpool won the title with

The most successful Villa manager of all time, Ron Saunders.

87 points against Ipswich, again second, gaining 83 points. Ron Saunders's Villa side had thus gained a bigger lead than Liverpool using the same points system. This has never been acknowledged by the media.

Nevertheless, the ability of the Villa players told its own story. England manager Ron Greenwood rightly gave caps to three of the best English players, Peter Withe – already a Championship medal winner with Nottingham Forest but never before capped – Tony Morley, and Gordon Cowans. Withe was capped immediately after the 1981 season was finished, Morley a year later when Villa were on their way to winning the European Cup, and Cowans making his breakthrough in 1983 when he had gained more European experience.

Withe made his England debut on 12 May 1981 at Wembley, playing in just about the toughest international imaginable for a first match, the Brazilians in full flow. Not suprisingly, England were beaten 1–0 and Withe did not score. He followed this up in two more matches in May at Wembley, against Wales and Scotland, again not scoring but being used primarily as a target man for other players to feed off. Perhaps significantly, England manager Ron Greenwood did not use him in the next two games, World Cup Qualifiers, but brought him back for a friendly against Norway, in which he was a late substitute for Paul Mariner. It seemed that Greenwood was testing Withe out as an alternative to Mariner. Suprisingly, he did not use the Villa combination of Morley on the wing and Withe in the centre, capping Morley twice without Withe and only in the Home International against Wales in April 1982 using both together. He clearly was not impressed. After a second pairing against Iceland, he took Withe to the 1982 World Cup and left Morley at home. But like Warnock in 2010, Withe did not get a game. It would be 1986 before a Villa player played in a World Cup Final – and then it was Steve Hodge, who would be remembered for all the wrong reasons.

After the World Cup, Mariner was preferred to Withe in the centre, but Morley gained two more caps before Bobby Robson, the new manager, decided he was not his winger of choice. Withe would, however, gain more caps in 1983. Robson's first move, however, was to call up Villa's creative midfielder Gordon Cowans, on 23 February 1983. Two games followed without any Villa players, then for three games in the early summer of the same year, Robson played Withe and Cowans in the same team.

Robson was a great admirer of the talented Cowans, and while he then dropped Withe he kept Cowans in the next three England games. For one of these, a friendly in Australia, Villa goalie Nigel Spink won his only cap. By the time matches resumed in the autumn of 1983, alas, Gordon Cowans had suffered a disasterous broken leg from which he would take over a year to recover. The next time he won a cap, he would be playing for the Italian club Bari. Peter Withe won a 10th cap substituting for Luther Blissett in October 1983, and a final 11th cap against Turkey in November 1984. Though England won 8–0 Withe did not score. After 11 games and only one goal, his England career was over. Nevertheless, the Saunders's players had put Villa back on the England map. With the 1986 World Cup looming and Villa back in the First Division, Villa players could think realistically about playing for England.

Paradoxically, the first player to benefit from this was Gordon Cowan's replacement. After recovering from his broken leg, Gordon moved to Italy to play in Serie A, following in Gerry Hitchens's footsteps. At this time Bobby Robson was looking for a player to cover for the England captain Brian Robson, who was injury prone. He looked first at Cowans, giving him his eighth cap against Egypt in January 1986. Gordon scored in a 4–0 victory and looked set fair, but two games later he was substituted on 53 minutes for Steve Hodge. Hodge did well enough to be selected for the next game, and it was clear Robson had decided Hodge would do the job. Villa would have a player in a World Cup Final at long

The Saunders ethic, total commitment. From left to right: Mark Jones, Des Bremner, Gordon Cowans, Denis Mortimer, Gary Williams, Ivor Linton, Peter Withe. Bremner, Cowans and Mortimer were the greatest Villa midfield trio in living memory.

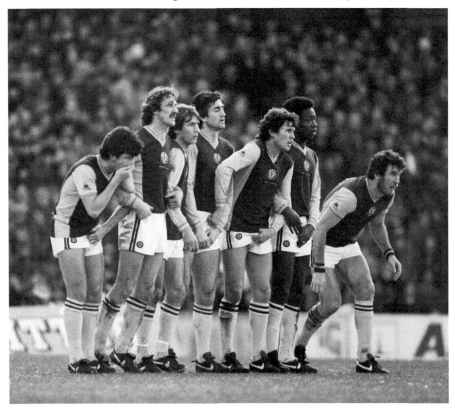

last. Hodge was not initially fully established in the England team, substituting for Ray Wilkins as well as Bryan Robson in the run up to the World Cup, but by Round Two he was fully established, gaining his eighth cap.

Alas, he will probably be best remembered for his role in the Hand of God goal by Maradonna. Hodge accidentally played Maradonna on side attempting a clearance, which he sliced badly to put the ball back into the penalty area. Maradonna ran at England goalie Shilton, the ball went into the back of the net, and England protested Maradonna had knocked it there with his hand: but the referee let it stand. The goal knocked England out of the competition. However, there were no recriminations because of a single mistake, and Hodge continued to play for England. Indeed, he could be considered first choice over Ray Wilkins. But after 11 caps, following the dismissal of the Villa manager who had signed him, Graham Turner, Hodge asked for a transfer away from Villa Park and was sold to Tottenham Hotspur. He continued his England career, ending up with 24 caps by the time he played his last match in 1991.

The eighties make Villa credible again

The 1980s re-established the credibility of Villa as a club of potential internationals. While the 35 years from 1946 to 1981 had only produced five internationals with a meagre haul of nine caps between them, the eight years to 1989 had produced another five internationals but this time with 37 caps between them, and in less than a quarter of the time. Villa was now seen as a club which could attract good players, and at its best able to spot youth potential and groom it. This was the Billy Walker and Gordon Cowans approach. The other Villa route to success was to find a less obvious talent and make it special, which was the Gerry Hitchens model. Villa were now about to prove its ability to find a major undeveloped talent and take it to the top, under manager, Graham Taylor.

David Platt's career overlapped with Gordon Cowans's, and in many ways they were two sides of the coin of Villa achievers. Gordon was the brilliant teenager who was destined for success from the start, and only needed to be given the right challenge as Villa coached him through from the youth team. Sadly, at the peak of his potential a broken leg prevented him from ever reaching the heights which had seemed to be his for the taking in the magic four seasons when Villa rose to the very top in Europe. David Platt was never seen as a brilliant prospect and almost drifted out of the game as a teenager after being rejected by Manchester United as having potential but not enough to be certain. He then proved them wrong by using the training offered at Crewe and Villa to break through as a brilliantly effective player. By the time his career ended, Platt was the most expensive player of his era.

Platt broke through in a Villa team that had just returned to the First Division under Graham Taylor. He himself was stunned when Villa contacted him to tell him he was called up for the England squad, not considering himself the equal of players like the brilliant but erratic Paul Gascoigne, but this worked to his benefit. He worked his passage, learning the trade of international footballer largely as a substitute in the games before the 1990 World Cup. He was taken to Italy to cover for better-known players, until with his eighth cap he was again called off the bench on 71 minutes of a 0–0 draw with Belgium. Only a win would take England through to the quarter-finals. With only a minute to go, Gascoigne floated a free kick over the Belgian wall. At which moment, Platt peeled off the wall, and with perfect timing hit the ball on the volley into the net and England were through. His career went into overdrive.

Though England did not win the World Cup, Platt made the midfield general role his own. When Graham Taylor took over from Bobby Robson, Gordon Cowans was recalled to play alongside Platt, perhaps to recreate the highly successful partnership they had established playing for the Villa. But this was impossible. While Platt continued to hold down his place, for Cowans the game had moved too far ahead. It was inevitable that Platt would move to Italy. In the late summer of 1991, he signed for Bari having won 22 caps while at Villa Park. No Villa fan begrudged his taking his chance, and his success following his transfer proved that Villa could be a springboard to international success.

Making waves in the nineties

Villa's record in the number of players who earned caps in the 1990s looks good on the surface – 10 players were picked for England. But it is less impressive when it is realised that six only won one cap. Kevin Richardson, Ugo Ehiogu, Stan Collymore, Dion Dublin, Lee Hendrie and Paul Merson only won one when with the Villa, though of course Paul Merson was near the end of his career with most of his caps behind him when he joined the club. Whether the lack of success for the others was due to a lack of ability or Villa's patchy form in a decade when they won two League Cups, came second twice, but never really established themselves, is a big question.

But what cannot be denied is the outstanding success of Gareth Southgate, who became one of the most successful players for England ever while wearing claret and blue. Gareth was an excellent, highly intelligent and well-organised central defender who stood out during an era of first-class English central defenders. His first cap was on 12 December 1995. He held his own when players like Sol Campbell and Tony Adams were at the peak of their form with England and Arsenal. Initially, he formed a partnership with Adams, gaining unwanted fame in his ninth game by missing the crucial penalty against Germany in the penalty shoot out in the 1996 European Championships.

It did not harm his career, and Southgate turned it into a joke in a TV pizza commercial where he wore a paper bag over his head. He played through the following World Cup Qualifiers. He then played in the 1998 World Cup. Terry Venables and Glenn Hoddle as England managers were big admirers, but Kevin Keegan was not as favourable. However, the European Championship failure in 2000, when Southgate played little part, worked in his favour and Keegan restored him to the squad. He fell out of favour when Sven-Goran Eriksson was appointed manager, but Eriksson did give him his 42nd cap as a Villa player when he substituted him for Martin Keown on 25 May 2001. He set a mark which will be very hard to beat both for appearances and quality and style of play.

Keegan gave Gareth Barry his breakthrough as a young player, in the early summer of 2000, and Barry won two further caps under Keegan, and two under caretaker managers Howard Wilkinson, and Peter Taylor. Sven-Goran Eriksson did not see Gareth Barry as part of his plans, despite trying him in two friendlies. Not till Martin O'Neill revived his career at Villa Park did Barry become first choice for the England squad. Eriksson did, however, favour Darius Vassell, who rewarded him for his first cap in February 2002 with a spectacular bicycle kick which earned England a draw and saved Eriksson's blushes. Over the next 26 months, Eriksson gave Vassell 22 caps, using him mainly as an impact sub whose speed and strength were very effective against tiring defences. His last game for England was as a substitute for Wayne Rooney, in a 2–2 draw in the European Championships of 2004. Sadly, it was clear that Rooney was the up-and-coming player for terrorising opposition defences.

Eriksson did not give any Villa players caps in the last years of his managership, and only when he quit after the defeat at the World Cup in the summer of 2006 did Villa begin to win caps again. This was in part due to the poor form of the team since the Cup Final of 2000, after which Villa retreated into middle table obscurity under John Gregory, Graham Taylor, who returned for a second period less successful than his first, and David O'Leary. Only when Martin O'Neill came to the club and renewed its fortunes did Villa players again begin to win caps, with four of his squad having won caps while playing for Villa – Gabriel Agbonlahor, Ashley Young, Emile Heskey and James Milner. In addition, Stephen Warnock was called into the England squad for South Africa after being signed by O'Neill and Gareth Barry returned to the national side under O'Neill.

The player who most benefitted from O'Neill's coaching was Gareth Barry, who became a regular under Steve McLaren and continued to be a regular till he left Villa for Manchester City in June 2009. McLaren also gave Ashley Young his first cap, on 16 October 2007, but it was not till the Capello era that Villa players began to get regular calls from the England camp.

The Capello era

When Fabio Capello became England manager on 6 February 2008 it was good news for England – Capello had no prejudice against players at Villa Park. He continued to pick Gareth Barry, whose outstanding form sadly led him to leave for the money bags of Manchester City in 2009, followed by James Milner in August 2010. In the run up to the World Cup in June 2010, Capello looked to Villa for players to take to South Africa. Emile Heskey, who joined Villa in January 2009, was tried, as were Milner (still a Villa Player), Ashley Young and Gabriel Agbonlahor. In the end, Heskey and Milner were on the plane for the World Cup – as was Stephen Warnock. Warnock was taken as cover for Ashley Cole at left-back, and was not to play.

This was not the case with Milner and Heskey. For the first time ever, Villa had two players in a World Cup Final – and three in the squad. Withe had been taken in 1982 but not played, Hodge, (1986), Platt (1990), Southgate (1998) and Vassell (2002) had all been taken and played. But for the first time, two players on the Villa staff would go to a World Cup and play.

Sadly, the campaign ended in tears. Heskey played well in the first game, a 1–1 draw against the USA, but Milner had to come off with a stomach virus. In the second game Heskey started but did not score in a truly awful England performance, a 0–0 draw against Algeria, and was never picked to start again. Milner came in for the third game and provided the cross for Defoe to score the winner against Slovenia. Milner started for the fourth game against the Germans, but could do little as England went down to their worst-ever World

Cup Finals defeat at 4–1. Heskey could do even less – he was brought on after 71 minutes when England had already conceded four. Only a miracle worker could have saved the situation.

After the disappointment of the 2010 World Cup. Capello had to start rebuilding – and it is clear he is looking to Villa Park as a key part of this process. Heskey retired from international football and Milner moved to Manchester City before the start of the 2010–11 season, but Ashley Young was in Capello's sights from the start. He only started one game in the period up to and including the Denmark game on 9 February 2011, that against the minnows of Montenegro, but played as substitute in four of the five other post-South Africa matches to this date. Against Denmark he opened his scoring account and, with Darren Bent playing from the start of the game, and now a Villa player, this bodes well for the future. In the same game against Denmark, Downing came on to make Villa's 71st cap – Darren Bent having become the 70th earlier in the game, and Stephen Warnock the 69th against France on 17 November 2010, it is very obvious that Fabio Capello knows the way to Villa Park.

Anyone who looks back at the history of Aston Villa realises it is a story of highs and lows. Hopefully the lows are behind us, but the basic lesson of Villa's history is very clear. Take nothing for granted, and keep ahead of the opposition. Villa did this in the early years, and became a world famous club. It did not do so for large parts of the 20th century, and the international record suffered from poor performances on the pitch and in the boardroom. It can also shoot itself in the foot, as the resignation of Martin O'Neill days before the start of the 2010–11 season shows is still sadly the case.

The history of the club shows that it can produce internationals for England – and other countries not dealt with in this book – but there are no certainties and only matching the best will do. After the Wilderness Years Villa got themselves back in contention in the 1980s and then almost lost it again. Currently the club is showing real potential but if the tradition laid down by Vaughton, Brown, Whateley and their colleagues back in the 1880s is to be upheld, the only path Villa can take is to set high standards – and then do even better.

Pantheon Players

ATHERSMITH, Charlie

Position: Outside-right
Born: Bloxwich, Staffordshire, 10 May 1872
Died: Shifnal, 18 September 1910
Career: Walsall Rd Council School; Bloxwich Wanderers; Bloxwich Strollers; Unity Gas Depot; ASTON VILLA (February 1891); Birmingham (June 1901); Grimsby Town (trainer, June 1907 to May 1909)

England
Caps: 12, Won: 9, Lost: 2, Drawn: 1, Goals: 3

In the 10 years Charlie Athersmith played for the Villa, he became one of the best players in his position in the country. His peak years were from 1897 to 1900 when he was first choice in his position for England. He started playing for Villa in 1890, and his talent was so obvious that he won his first cap on 15 March 1892, but Billy Bassett of West Bromwich Albion kept him out of the England team five years. It was not till 20 February 1897 that Athersmith finally replaced Bassett as first choice on England's right wing. Bassett had won 16 caps, scoring eight times proving his great ability. The Villa man had no choice but to wait, but meanwhile established himself as a great club player.

His massive role in Villa's most successful team of all time in domestic competitions is beyond doubt. Athersmith won five Championship medals – 1894, 1896, 1897, 1899 and 1900 – and two FA Cup-winners' medals, in 1895 and 1897. He made 311 senior appearances, scoring 86 goals, and was ever present in the historic double-winning side of 1896–97. It is remarkable he is in the 300 club of appearances given the limited number of games Villa played in the Victorian era.

The history books alas do not explain what made him such a good player. He was speedy, and some accounts make him sound like the Gabriel Agbonlahor of the 1890s. Charlie Johnstone, the ex-Villa player who joined the Villa board

in 1896 when Athersmith was at his peak, recalled in his obituary of Athersmith in the *Sporting Mail* that the Villa team of 1894–97 was the fastest in the League and Athersmith led the way. He challenged Johnstone and another trainer to a race, giving them a 5yd headstart in an 80yd race, and beat them. But Athersmith was not just about running fast. Johnstone also saw him as a team player of great accuracy and foresight, particularly in working with John Devey.

Athersmith's achievements with Villa paid off when his form in the double-winning season made him the obvious choice to replace Bassett. He scored in his second match, a 6–0 victory against the Irish. Following this, he was an ever present for the next eight games, missed one, then returned for a final two games in 1900. He was not a prolific scorer with only three goals, but given that England scored 46 goals in the 12 games he played in, he was a key part of a successful goalscoring machine. One of the games was a second 13-goal thrashing of the Irish in 1899, when the famous G.O. Smith of the Corinthians captained the team. Even taking away this fluke result, England averaged three goals a game when Athersmith played, so clearly he worked his shift. In an era before cameras captured football matches evidence about players is always vague, but the eye-witness accounts make it clear that, like Agbonlahor, there was more to his game than merely great pace.

He left Villa in 1901 for Birmingham City, helping Blues finish runners up in Division Two, and went on the unsanctioned Tagg and Campbell tour of Germany in 1905, for which he was banned. It was a sad end to a great career. In addition to his full caps he played twice for an England XI and represented the Football League nine times 1894–1901.

Charlie Johnstone on Athersmith, *Sporting Mail*, 24 September 1910.
'In spite of his "innocent jollity" Charlie was an apostle of fitness and his example in this direction was of great assistance to the trainer. But it was his brilliant play as outside right which will cause him to live in our memories. Very quick in gathering a ball and getting into his stride, he seemed to divine intuitively the exact position for receiving Devey's pass. Then came the electrifying rush down the wing, almost invariably culminating in an accurate and beautifully timed centre to Hodgett's foot or Wheldon's head. There have been cleverer and more brilliant dribblers, but I doubt if a more effective outside right ever played than Athersmith.'

Villa News & Record, 4 February 1920, pages 10–11.
'Charles of the fair locks and long legs was the quickest to get away from the ruck and the hardest to overtake that any football crowds have ever seen. He was wonderfully consistent, too; and though of course he had his "off" days, nine times out of ten the great right winger gave us displays – and especially

when John Devey was his partner – that sent us away full of admiration for the prowess and pace of the performer.

'He had the gifts of speed and skill, and for the first few years of his football career he feared no foe; but the in later seasons he was more apt to take care of himself, and avoid the shocks which once fell so liberally to his share. Indeed, he had a great deal more than his fair share of them, for the baser sort of professional "went for" the man rather than the ball, because they knew that once he had passed them all hope of catching him had fled.

'I remember a particularly brilliant game he played against the Corinthians in London, the year the Villa won the Cup from the Albion by a goal to nothing – about the middle nineties. He was 'the bright particular star' of that game, and the Londoners cheered him again and again for the way in which he raced away from his opponents.

'His ability did not consist solely of his pace and accuracy in sweeping the ball across the goal mouth, for he was a fine dribbler, a deft passer and some of those swift slanting shots of his, which had a curiously correct way of finding their billet in the far corner of the net, were deadly things for a goalkeeper...he never developed swank or side, and he was one of the giants of the long list of men who have helped make Aston Villa the great powerful club that it is.'

Villa News & Record, 1 September 1906.
'One of the fleetest right wingers of his time. With a working partner he was well nigh irresistible. Great at touch line play and centred with unerring precision. In consequence of his speed, has been penalised for offside play times out of number by unobservant and at times incompetent referees. Posseses a unique record in international matches.'

COWANS, Gordon Sidney

Position: Left midfield
Born: Cornforth, County Durham, 27 October 1958
Career: ASTON VILLA (apprentice, July 1974, professional, August 1976); Bari (£450,000, 1985); ASTON VILLA (£250,000, 2 July 1988); Blackburn Rovers (£200,000, November 1991); ASTON VILLA (free transfer, July 1993); Derby County (£80,000, February 1994); Wolves (£20,000, December 1994); Sheffield

United, (free, December 1995); Bradford City (free, July 1996); Stockport County (free, March 1997); Burnley (free, reserve-team player-coach, August 1997–May 1998); ASTON VILLA (assistant manager-coach, August 1998). Worked in the Academy with the young players until 10 September 2010 when appointed first-team coach.

England

Caps: 10, Won: 6, Lost: 0, Drawn: 4, Goals: 2. (Villa 8, Bari 2)

Gordon 'Sid' Cowans is the the most deeply rooted of Villa Greats in the recent history of the club. While he has travelled to a number of clubs in search of fortune and experience, he has always returned to the Villa. He has a very special place in the history of the club, and the story is not yet over. As a player he lies second in the 300 club, but unlike the other two in the top three, Charlie Aitken number one and Billy Walker number three, he did not spend the whole of his top-flight career at the Villa. He left, but he kept coming back. To amass that number of appearances over three separate playing periods at the club is remarkable. He was appointed first-team coach in September 2010.

The Villa connection started very early in his life, when he was 10 years old. Tommy Docherty and Vic Crowe were jointly responsible for the success of the Villa Youth scheme, but it was chief scout Neville Briggs who saw him playing for Newlands School in the Mansfield district and started chatting to his pitman father. The Villa management became so convinced that he was a vital talent that they contacted the Physical Education teacher at his school and invited the school to send pupils to see a match at Villa Park. Thus, his first experience of Villa Park was seeing the second match of the first season in the Third Division – a defeat!

Despite the club's interest, when Villa offered Cowans a schoolboy contract at 13 his father declined, as other clubs were also interested. But Villa were absolutely determined to sign such an exceptional talent, and had an ace in the hole. They offered Mr Cowans the job of running the youth hostel if Gordon moved to Birmingham. As he had been working in the mines for 25 years, the chance of leaving the pits was too good to miss and he and his son came to Birmingham when Gordon finished school. In the modern world, executives do not go down coal mines to sign players as Fred Rinder did for Steve Smith. Players are signed earlier, and with a different career pattern.

Cowans joined a promising bunch of youngsters. Manager Crowe had laid the basis of Ron Saunders great teams of the late nineteen seventies though he did not benefit from this. Cowans made his first-team debut as a sub on 7 February 1976. This was the match after Charlie Aitken had signed off – continuing a chain of long player appearances going back to Frank Broome through Johnny Dixon and Charlie Aitken, the so-called Lion's baton. On September 1977 he played his first full match, but he was still too young to be

a regular and the day after the match, against Norwich City in the League Cup, Saunders signed Alex Cropley to be the midfield flair player.

Cowans was learning his trade as a fringe player in the first of the great Saunders's teams, the 1977 League Cup-winning side, and he was not in the Wembley team, but he was good enough to be in the two replay sides when Cropley was injured (McColl p.92). He was also in the UEFA Cup team in March 1978 to play Cruyff's Barcelona, again deputising for Cropley who had had his leg broken against WBA the previous December. He said of the two-legged game 'It was nice for us as players to get the chance to play against a different style of football and to pit our wits and our own game against continentals. Playing against Barcelona and Johan Cryuff is an outstanding memory. At the time he was the best player in the world and, as a lad, he had always been one of my heroes' (McColl p.95).

Gordon was developing his skills at the top level, but 1978 was the effective end of the second Saunders team, and the club entered a crisis period as Saunders fell out with a number of key players, who left over the next 18 months, including Andy Gray, Gordon Smith, John Gidman, and Brian Little, while the club was hit with injuries to key players including Gordon. It was remarkable that Saunders kept his job, particularly as there was boardroom turmoil leading to Ron Bendall becoming chair in November 1979. In the midst of all this, Gordon Cowans kept developing and in 1980 was voted PFA Young Player of the Year.

Despite the turmoil behind the scenes, Ron Saunders survived as manager by keeping the club in the top half of the table each season. Saunders rebuilt the team for what was to be the greatest side for nearly a century. In the 1980–81 season only 14 players were used in the Championship team. Of the 14, Gordon Cowans was one of seven players who, astonishingly, were ever present, never in disciplinary trouble, never injured – a tribute to Saunders's coaching and their fitness and self discipline.

Cowans experienced even more success in the 1981–82 season, when Villa were back in Europe but this time for the European Cup. The UEFA Cup had taught some lessons, but for most players this was unknown territory. However, the squad, with very little recognition at international level was tight knit and supportive, and seven of the team had played in the UEFA run of 1978, including Gordon Cowans. Nevertheless this was sketchy preparation for a sudden death competition – unlike today, when a team can lose a couple of games and succeed, the old competition of four two-legged games meant that even one loss could be fatal.

However, with only nine games in the competition, the large squads of today were not needed. Luckily, Villa had few injuries, and none to Gordon Cowans, Despite his slight build, Sid coped with the challenges of football with resilience – as long as they were fair. In picking up his European champions' medal he showed exceptional qualities as an attacking midfield player. He also had remarkable stamina. The ever-present record of Gordon Cowans remains astonishing to this day. Between 1979 and 1983 Cowans did not miss a single game in any competition, winning League Championship, European Cup, and European Super Cup medals. He had matured into a very fine player indeed

When he took part in the 1982 Super Cup victory, it was clear he had the qualities needed for the England team. While Ron Greenwood would not pick him in the run up to the 1982 World Cup, Bobby Robson who replaced him was an admirer and once England had qualified for the European Cup, picked him on 23 February 1983 to play against Wales. During the Championship season, Robson had described Cowans as 'potentially the most compelete footballer and midfield man in English football'. He awarded Cowans six more caps in 1983, against Hungary, Northern Ireland, Scotland and three in the summer tour of Australia. But by the next international, in September, the sky fell in.

On 18 August 1983 in a pre-season warm-up match against FA America of Mexico, Andreus Manso smashed Cowans leg with a reckless tackle. He himself thinks that 'he intended me harm' (Hickman p.157) and went over the top with intent. If so, he succeeded. Cowans started the season in a hospital bed, ruled out for the season. He would eventually come back and to form, unlike Gary Shaw who was injured four games into the 1983–84 season and never recovered. But for Gordon Cowans, while he did come back in 1984–85 recovering full fitness took time. Playing for England was out of the question while he recovered.

He did recover, however, and played the whole season sufficiently well to attract interest from abroad, Bari, of Italian Serie A, bid for him and Paul Rideout. While he was abroad there was more behind the scenes trouble at Villa as Tony Barton followed Ron Saunders out the club and new managers Graham Turner and then Billy McNeil failed to stop a steady slide which would end in relegation. However Italy was not productive either. Gordon broke his leg again shortly after arriving in Italy, but fortunately not as badly as before. However

Bari were relegated to Serie B at the end of the 1985–86 season, but Gordon Cowans had returned to playing and once again atracted attention. He was called up by Bobby Robson for two friendlies, against Egypt on 29 January and the USSR on 26 March, as Robson pondered his midfield options.

England had already qualified, and Robson had seven months to consider his options. Alongside Kevin Keegan the England manager was likely to call up his

Newcastle colleagues, Peter Beardsley and Chris Waddle, but Robson needed a reserve midfield general as Bryan Robson, his captain, was injury prone. Robson gave Cowans two more caps in warm-up games against Egypt and the USSR in January and March 1986. Alas, for Gordon Cowans, Bobby Robson chose Steve Hodge to go to the World Cup. The irony was that Hodge, was playing for Aston Villa, and essentially replaced Gordon Cowans for both club and country. Cowans was coming up to 28 and appeared to have reached the peak of his career. However, a return to Villa gave him the chance to return to the limelight.

He returned to Villa in the summer of 1988. Graham Taylor had steadied the Villa ship and achieved promotion in the 1987–88 season. In rebuilding for a return to the top flight he considered Cowans, and flew over to Italy to see him. Chris Nicholl, the former Villa captain, offered him a return back home with Southampton, but when Taylor put a contract before him, the decision was inevitable. He could not know this, but he was about to enjoy a partnership which would make his second coming as memorable as the great days of the Saunders teams.

The 1988–89 season was difficult for the Villa and for Gordon Cowans, readjustments coming thick and fast. But in David Platt, Cowans found an inspirational partner. While Platt, a young player just signed from Crewe with raw potential, would joke his left foot was never as good as Cowan's he was in fact the ideal complement to the left-footed veteran, a right-sided attacker who played the same role as target man for Cowan's inch-perfect passes as Tony Morley had in the League Championship side. In his autobiography, Platt gave credit to Cowans for achieving England status. He had certainly gained immensely from Gordon Cowan's passes putting him through on goal, which on Platt's estimate took place on average three times per game.

The partnership was the key to two seasons of survival and development under Graham Taylor, the first establishing Villa back in the top flight, the second pushing on to a serious challenge for the title, which led to a second-place finish and established Graham Taylor as the bright new manager of the moment. Taylor was the obvious choice for the England job after the 1990 World Cup, but it was not obvious that he would turn to Gordon Cowans. Yet this was what he did on 14 November 1990 against Eire. Perhaps Taylor thought the partnership with Platt would work at England level. It did not. At the age of 32, Gordon could not stage a come back, and this was his last cap. In his 10 games for England, he was never on the losing side.

Ten caps for a player as talented as Gordon Cowans did not reflect his true ability. What would have happened had he not suffered the outragous assault which broke his leg in 1983 is impossible to tell. But in 1983 he was established as an England player having played five internationals in a row through to June – and when the matches resumed in October of that year, he was out for a year with his leg broken. His career never recovered at international level, his moment had passed. But for Villa, in the second coming with David Platt, he confirmed his reputation as one of the greatest players in the club's history.

Platt on Cowans:

David Platt cites his famous goal against Inter Milan in the 1990–91 UEFA Cup campaign, saying 'A long clearance by goalkeeper Nigel Spink was knocked back by Gordon Cowans to Tony Cascarino. He spotted me running from a deep position, and expertly lifted the ball over the defence to run on to, control and place convincingly past Zenga…I received a great deal of glory for the way I finished that move off, but for me the best part was Sid's pass. It is my firm belief that Sid helped me get into the England team and helped to keep me there. Of the 68 goals I scored for Aston Villa, he was responsible for making approximately seventy per cent of them. His range of passing with either foot was unbelievable: this, coupled with his vision, meant he invariably gave me three efforts on goal per game. During my time at Villa I was once asked what my ambition was. I joked that it was to make a run that Gordon Cowans did not see.'

Achieving the goal: An Autobiography p.98.

HARDY, Samuel

Position: Goalkeeper
Born: Newbould Verdun, Derbyshire, 25 August 1883
Died: Chesterfield, 24 November 1966
Career: Newbould White Star (July 1901); Chesterfield (professional, April 1903); Liverpool (£500, October 1905); Villa (May 1912); Nottingham Forest (August 1921–May 1925)

England

Caps: 21, Won: 12, Lost: 4, Drawn: 5, Goals: 0

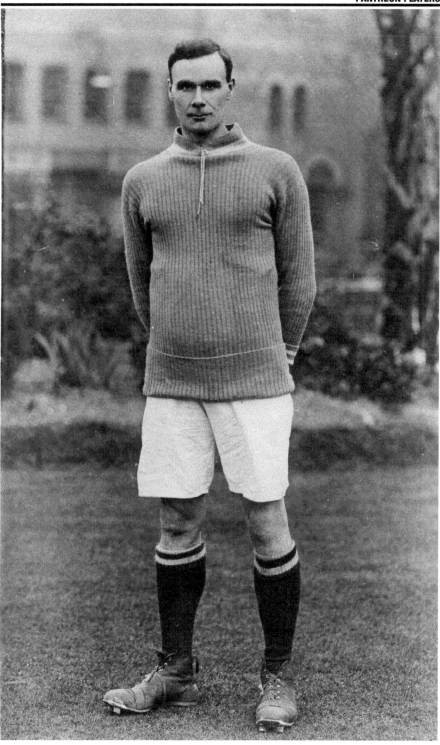

One of the top English footballers of the 20th century, Hardy was signed by Liverpool from Chesterfield despite conceding six goals against the Merseysiders, his ability being abundantly clear even playing behind a very dodgy defence. He played for Liverpool for nearly seven years, winning a Championship medal in 1906. However, Liverpool declined and after the club finished fourth from bottom in 1912 Hardy moved to Villa. It is a sign of Villa's pre-eminence in the English game that they could sign a premier England goalkeeper from Liverpool, a club which had won the League in 1905 and 1906 – though Liverpool were struggling to stay in the First Division.

Hardy almost immediately repaid Villa's move, saving Villa in the 1913 FA Cup quarter-final against Spurs almost single handedly. Then in the Final he had to go off for 10 minutes, Harrop deputising, but returned to guide the club to a winning scoreline. He was at his peak in 1913 despite being 30 – goalies get better with age up to 40 – and though his career was interrupted by the Great War he returned to win another Cup medal with Villa in 1920.

Villa had found a natural successor to William George, who he has, perhaps unfairly, overshadowed. Sadly his career was interrupted by the war, but he played 239 games for Liverpool, 183 senior matches for Villa in a war disrupted career, and 109 games for Notts Forest to add to the 70 games he played for Chesterfield. An impressive record. However, he had not become first-choice England goalkeeper easily.

From 16 April 1907, to 4 April 1908 he was tried with two other 'keepers for the England job. By February 1909, when he won his fifth cap, he held his place and he went on to win eight caps in succession before losing his place. Reginald Wilkinson and Ronald Scattergood were then tried, but he returned and kept a clean sheet against Scotland on 5 April 1913 and finally became the accepted goalkeeper.

He had won five caps as a Villa player and was firmly established as England 'keeper when war broke out and football was suspended. Thus, by spring 1914 he was established as first choice for Villa and England. How many caps he would have won if the war had not then stopped international matches can only be guessed at, but when internationals restarted in 1919 Hardy was first choice again. In 1920 he was still at his peak and only in 1921, after 15 years at the very top and approaching 40 years of age, did Villa transfer him to Nottingham Forrest in the second division.

Eyewitness accounts speak of his reliability and technical skill. At the time of the 1913 FA Cup Final, the *Villa News & Record* praised his high level of skill.

After the war his abilities remained unaffected. Following a match against Arsenal, the editor of the *Villa News & Record* commented:

'Quite the outstanding feature of the Villa match at Highbury last Saturday was the brilliant goalkeeping of Sam Hardy, who gave one of the most outstanding exhibitions of custodianship in a long and honourable career. It did not matter a jot how, where,or when the shot came – and there were a good many – Sam was always in the right spot, and we never saw a finer example of what is euphemistically called "intelligent anticipation". There were several "big wigs" of the Association present, and it was the unanimous opinion that Sam Hardy is still *facile princeps* (easily the first) between the sticks.'

More importantly, his fellow professionals rated him highly. In his autobiography, Billy Walker wrote of the lessons he learnt as a young forward coming through the ranks by the veteran 'keeper: Hardy did not operate by instinct – he thought about his game. And in case a Villa man might be seen as biased, it is even more impressive that when the England international and journalist Charles Buchan wrote his autobiography he featured Hardy.

Buchan selected two ideal teams from the players he had played with or against in the period after World War One. One team was drawn before the change in the offside law in 1925, the other after. In the pre 1925 era, Buchan considered Sam Hardy to be the greatest goalkeeper and he duly made him first-choice goalie.

When Hardy was dropped by England in 1921, his non selection caused controversy, with the Athletic News saying Hardy was 'still the finest custodian' but still had not been picked. Even at 38 Hardy was considered to be the best English goalie. His reputation has endured as one of the greatest English goalkeepers of all time. His record of 21 appearances between 16 February 1907 and 10 April 1920 puts him 13th in the all-time list. Only David James of the Villa group of goalies has done better.

At the end of the 20th century he was voted one of the League's 100 greatest players.

Athletic News, 1921

'England has played 24 players in the three matches, (ie Home Internationals, TF) including three goalkeepers, five backs, seven half-backs and nine forwards.... It may be urged that the dearth of talented players is the cause of so much vacillation.... Even so it is difficult to understand why three goalkeepers should have been chosen – and not one of these Hardy, still the finest custodian. In fact, the cynical might say that Hardy is the one man of international rank in the country, and then the selectors omit him against Scotland because Gough is 'entitled' to a cap, because Mew, the other goalkeeper who went to South Africa, was chosen to appear against Ireland. This surely is fatuity. Gough is no doubt an excellent custodian on his day. Unfortunately Saturday was not his day'. (Scotland had just beaten England 3–0).'

Villa News & Record (23 April 1913 p.547)

'[Hardy] saves difficult shots more easily than any other goalkeeper living, never appearing to be at full stretch to get to the ball. Hardy is just about the ideal goalkeeper. His remarkable intuition is founded upon constant watching of the positions of players and an experience that tells him to which part of the goal-mouth a forward must shoot...To realise how good Hardy is you must watch his movements before a shot is made. While forwards are dribbling and manoeuvring for an opening through which to shoot you will see Hardy stealing (not skipping and jumping, as is the case with the goalkeeper who is overanxious…) from place to place, but always well balanced for anything, whether it is the upward spring to the high shot, the downward dive to the ball that is low and wide, or for the catching and hugging of the ball when the rush of the opponent is so well timed that a shoulder charge must be resisted. The most extraordinary thing about Hardy's play is the fact that he does great things easily'.

Billy Walker, *Socccer in the Blood*, 1960, pp.29–30

'I have one poignant personal reccollection...In a practice game before the season started I was playing for the reserves against the first team...I went through the defence and lifted up my head to see where to shoot. I saw Sam move towards his left-hand post and straight away I shot to the opposite post as hard as I could. When my head came up I saw Sam standing at the post, just catching the ball. His husky voice came to me as he said 'send a postcard, send a postcard.

'At half time I went to him and asked "Mr Hardy (we called the senior professionals Mister), what did you mean about sending a postcard?" He asked me, "Where was I when you picked your head up?" I said to him, "At the left post, so I shot for the right post". So Sam said "What do you think I stood at the other post for?" In other words, he made me shoot where he wanted me to!'

HITCHENS, Gerry (Gerald Archibald)

Position: Centre-forward
Born: Rawnsley, Staffordshire, 8 October 1934
Died: Wrexham, North Wales, 13 April 1983
Career: Kidderminster Harriers (August 1953); Cardiff City (£1500, January 1955); Villa (£22,500, December 1957); Inter-Milan (£60,000, June 1961); Torino (£50,000, November 1962); Atalanta of Bergamo (£25,000, June 1965); Cagliari of Sardinia (£5,000, June 1967); Worcester City (November 1969); Merthyr Tydfil (September 1971); retired May 1972 and went into business in Pontypridd. Died on the football pitch in a friendly match.

England
Caps: 7, Won: 4, Lost: 3, Drawn: 0, Goals: 5

Gerry Hitchens is one of the forgotten players not just of Villa, but of English football history. Massively successful in England and Italy, he should be remembered as a pioneer of the international movement of British players – something which helped to abolish the maximum wage, and make the football world a global one. Instead, he has been almost forgotten outside Villa circles.

He was not the first British player to go to Italy successfully – John Charles had already done that. But Charles was regarded as a genius. Hitchens's success was of a less-gifted player, but one who showed it was not unusual to be able to play abroad. With talent, hard work, and a willingness to fit in on and off the pitch, British players could move abroad successfully.

The careers of players like Paul Gascoigne, Gary Lineker, Tony Cascarino and Villa's Gordon Cowans and David Platt owe an massive debt to a modest man who had nothing to be modest about. There have been technically superior players at Villa. There have certainly been players who played more matches,

and made more impact on the club. But Gerry Hitchens is historically the single most important player ever to appear for Aston Villa. Without intending to make waves, Gerry Hitchens showed that doing your job well can change the world.

Hitchens and the Villa

Gerry Hitchens's career is a classic Villa story of talent, hard work and success. Villa rarely have the superstars in any era. What makes for a successful Villa player at any level is a core of talent, the work ethic to have the talent develop to its maximum, and the ability to exploit the talent to win the respect of those who watch from the terraces. Villa do not attract players with the extravagant talent of a George Best or a Paul Gascoigne. But their successful players have their feet on the ground even while they reach for the stars. Gerry Hitchens embodied all the qualities of a classic Villa player, a raw talent which he and the club developed to great success.

Within this broad profile of a classic Villa player there are two types of career – the players who come back and the players who escape. Vaughton, Devey, Houghton and Cowans are examples of players who return, their hearts being at the club. Walker, Platt, Danny Blanchflower and Gerry Hitchens are examples of players who move on. Yet without their time at the Villa, their later success could never have happened. Few careers show this better than that of Gerry Hitchens, the working-class miner from Shropshire who rose to Inter Milan and the 1962 World Cup in Chile – via the Villa.

The story of Hitchens is the story of a man striving for success. It also shows wider changes in the game of football, the career developing outside England. Nowadays, this is taken for granted, but at the time it was very uncertain whether English players could survive on the Continent. Hitchens is significant because at the time of his transfer to Italy people like Joe Baker, Denis Law and Jimmy Greaves came back and it was thought that British players could not settle. His success contributed to the abolition of the maximum wage as clubs came to fear losing their best talent to clubs abroad.

Although Hitchens stay abroad was successful, and proved that the English style of play was not incompatible with Italian catenaccio, the significance of what he achieved was overlooked. Precisely because he stayed abroad and missed the World Cup triumph in 1966, he has largely been forgotten outside Villa Park. His story should be better known.

The Background

Gerry Hitchens was born on 8 October 1934 in Rawnsley, near Cannock in the South Staffordshire coalfield – not far from Hednesford, where Fred Rinder had signed Steve Smith from down a pit shaft 40 years earlier. However, there was little sign in his early years that he would achieve massive success.

The family moved to Highley, a small mining village in Shropshire where his father got a job down the pit and Gerry went to the local school. He was not academic and left at 15 years of age to join his father underground. He soon scored goals for the Miners team as centre-forward. He was big and strong and one season scored 90 goals. Scouts from big clubs showed a little interest, but only non-League Kidderminster Harriers moved to sign him. He signed as a professional, on £2 per week, and played his first game as a pro on 12 September 1953.

He was not quite 19 – late to start a professional football career. This was not a tale of overnight success, but Gerry had two characteristics: he scored goals at whatever level he played at, and he worked at his game. On 22 January 1955 he scored before a scout from Cardiff City, and three days later he was signed by the Welsh club for £1,500. In 18 months as amateur and pro he had scored 20 goals in 40 appearances – enough for Cardiff to sign him at 20 years old as understudy to centre-forward Trevor Ford.

Making his reputation – the Cardiff Years

Gerry made the leap from non-League to the First Division successfully, so much so that he was quickly playing alongside the controversial Trevor Ford. Unlike Ford, who was constantly involved in arguments, Gerry Hitchens simply gave 100 per cent on the pitch and scored regularly – a managers dream. By the end of his first full season, 1955–56, he was the club's top scorer with 28 goals in all competitions, winning his first medal, in a Welsh Cup victory. He was now a recognised player at the top level and was called up for an FA tour of South Africa – which did not earn full caps but showed he was a promising player. He took his opportunity, scoring 17 goals in 12 games.

Off the pitch, Gerry had met his future wife, Meriel Jones, a 17-year-old student at the local college. It was November 1955. Gerry was just 21, with an engaging personality, and charmed both Meriel and her parents. The polite, hard-working and well-balanced character who was dating their daughter seemed to Meriel's parents an ideal son-in-law. It was inevitable he would marry Meriel. They finally wed on 27 October 1958, by which point Gerry had moved to the Villa. This uncomplicated man was now contented and had a focus for his life in his family.

His second season with Cardiff, 1956–57, was successful for Gerry but not for Cardiff. He was picked for the England Under-23 team in September, but despite him scoring 21 goals in the League, Cardiff were relegated from the top flight. Life in the Second Division was not an option, and when the club failed

to make a good start he became an asset the club could cash in to rebuild for the future. It was Eric Houghton, the legendary ex-England international now managing the club, who made a successful offer. On 22 December 1957 Hitchens moved to Villa Park.

Making his reputation – the Aston Villa Years

There was no doubting his scoring record – he had scored 57 goals in 108 games for Cardiff, better than a goal every two games. But there were still doubts about his technical ability at the highest level. Indeed, many commentators saw Hitchens as a strong physical player with pace, but who scored goals by instinct rather than intent and was a poor header of the ball. Hitchens was certainly a natural goalscorer and 11 goals in the first 22 games of his half season showed that he had not lost his scent for goal by moving back to the Midlands. Alas, the next season, Hitchens's first full season for the Villa, saw him back in a struggling team as the defence leaked goals.

Just as with Cardiff, Hitchens found himself in a relegation struggle. Eric Houghton's failure led to his sacking on 19 November 1958 and a new manager, Joe Mercer, was appointed. It was a turning point for Hitchens. Mercer admired him, but also saw how his talent could be improved by coaching. Mercer could not stop the club being relegated, and spent the next season getting Villa back up. Hitchens's goals helped get Villa back up.

But he was still an unrefined player and in preparing for the return to Division One in the summer of 1960 Mercer and his assistant Dick Taylor worked to improve his raw skills. Their work was rewarded. Hitchens added ball control and anticipation to strength and pace. He was a far more potent centre-forward when he returned to Division One in August 1960.

The improvement was noticed by expert observers. After Villa acheved a 5–1 victory over Manchester City, the legendary City goalkeeper Bert Trautmann who had seen Hitchens put two of the five past him, 'What a player he has become. I remember him in his Cardiff days, and what a change there has been since then!' (*The Gerry Hitchens Story*, Simon Goodyear, p.59) Villa finished ninth at the end of the 1960–61 season and there was press clamour for Hitchens to be selected for England. The selectors decided to stick with Jimmy Greaves and Bobby Smith, and their decision was vindicated in a 9–3 victory over the Scots on 15 April, the two strikers sharing five goals between them. Hitchen's route into the England team seemed to be barred.

Hitchens scoring on his debut for England against Mexico, 1961.

Nevertheless, the first season back in the First Division had been a great success. He won the *Birmingham Mail* Player of the Year award, voted by fans across the West Midlands, beating Vic Crowe, Don Howe, Bobby Robson, Jimmy Dugdale and Ron Flowers in an open contest. He also won the Aston Villa Supporters Club Player of the Year award. It was clear that he was enormously popular and the selectors could not ignore this. He was selected for the England FA team to play the Scottish FA and though this was not a full cap the signs were good.

Villa had a planned tour of Russia in May. The League Cup Final, a two-legged affair, was postponed to allow this to go ahead, but with England having an continental tour planned, it was clearly sensible for Hitchens to wait at home to see if an England call would come. Walter Winterbottom, the England manager, finally made the call and Gerry won his first cap on 10 May 1961 against Mexico. He played well enough for Winterbottom to select him for the continental tour which followed.

Meanwhile, he was attracting attention from Italy. Club chair Chris Buckley called him and Meriel into Villa Park to tell them that Internazionale Milan were interested in signing him. Gerry asked to postpone a decision until after he had come back from the continent. However, when he played in Italy, scoring two of England's goals in a 3–2 friendly in Rome, interest from Inter became red hot. AC Milan, who famously shared the San Siro stadium with Inter, were signing Jimmy Greaves and though Greaves was trying to pull out of the agreement he had made with agent Gigi Peronance, English footballers were the current fashion and Inter wanted their own Englishman.

Although it was a pioneering move – at that time only John Charles at Juventus had made a successful transition to Italian football – and the family had two young children, with wealth far beyond what they could expect in England dangled before them, there was really no choice. When Gerry had been asked once by a reporter how he would spend £50 – the top English football wage was £20 with a £4 win bonus – he replied 'I would buy the wife a new dress, get a babysitter, and have a super night out – theatre, the lot' (*The Gerry Hitchens Story*, Simon Goodyear, p.53). A move to Italy would mean this would no longer be a pipedream, but a weekly possibility.

On 15 June 1961 Gerry Hitchens signed for Inter in a deal worth £85,000 for Villa and, it was rumoured, a signing on fee of £10,000 – big money in 1961. The signing meant he missed the League Cup Final over two legs, and was denied a medal when Villa won. The decision upset him – he had scored 11 of Villa's 26 goals on the way to the Final – but the Villa stage of his career was now over. He had been honed by the Villa coaches into an international class player, and as with Cardiff and Kidderminster, having created an asset the club cashed in. He had no idea how his future would develop, but he had dedicated himself to pushing his career as far as it would go. He was now an international player in more ways than one.

Gerry Hitchens's achievement in making the England team and securing the move to Inter is remarkable in many ways. He had been a late developer, only starting as a pro at age 19. He had played in struggling teams, twice being relegated. His two years at Cardiff had never seen the team hit the heights, though he did gain his only domestic medal in the Welsh Cup. The year in a struggling Villa team under Eric Houghton did little for him and, although he had toured South Africa in summer 1956 for the FA, he had done little in the years to 1960 to suggest he would make the transition to full international. It was the work done on the training ground in the summer of 1960 which made the difference. Credit has to go to Joe Mercer and Dick Taylor in finally honing his technical skills so that when he returned to the First Division in 1960–61 he was a player who could be considered as good as the best. He was now 26, experienced, strong and pacy, but with the ability to outfox defenders.

Yet he had still not won anything more than a Welsh Cup medal, and he was even denied the League Cup medal he felt he deserved, because he did not play in the Final as he had gone to Italy. Few people outside Villa Park, where he was a folk hero, or the observers of club football in the backrooms of top football clubs, ever appreciated that this was more than just an instinctive goalscorer. He was certainly that, as his record showed. He scored 96 goals in 160 League and Cup appearances for the Villa between 1957–61, a scoring ratio of better than a goal every two games (a gaol every 1.66 games, beating the record of the other goalscoring Villa giant of his era Tony Hateley (Hateley scored 86 goals in 148 games 1963–67 – a 1.72 ratio). He left Villa with Villa fans wondering what might have been as the club entered the worst decade in its history. But Hitchens now operated as an England international and a player for Inter Milan. He had no time to look back, and no reason to do so.

Hitchens and the 1962 World Cup

Winterbottom took Hitchens to South America for the World Cup in Chile. The Hitchens-Greaves partnership had promise, and they played in a 4–0 victory against Peru in which Hitchens did not score, and the Round One match of the Cup in which neither striker scored. Hitchens was left out for the 3–1 victory against Argentina, and the 0–0 draw which was enough to take them through to the quarter-final match against Brazil. Hitchens was picked to play against the eventual winners. England could not cope with Brazilian flair, though Gerry Hitchens did score England's only goal as they were knocked out 3–1. Hitchens never played again for England. But his last international game saw him on the same score sheet as the Brazilian superstar Garrincha. Finishing his international career on the same sheet as the Little Bird was a massive achievement.

But it was a premature end for Hitchens and England. The new manager, Alf Ramsay, disliked players based outside England, but for Hitchens it hardly mattered. His priority was to play good football and look after his family. Life in Italy, where he played two years for Inter, followed by three years playing for Torino, two for Atalanta, and three for Cagliari, enabled him to achieve his goals. It was not till 1970 that he returned to England, to play non-League football for Worcester. By the time he returned English football was starting to realise Alf Ramsay was living in the past. But it was too late for Hitchens.

People who knew better realised that Hitchens had been right to go to Italy, but he had been forgotten. As someone who knew him well and had failed in Italy, Jimmy Greaves, rightly commented later, 'he spent so long playing in Italy that he is overlooked when people start talking about the outstanding British players of the 1960s' (*The Gerry Hitchens Story* p10). He only won seven caps. It should have been far more. But the real importance of Gerry Hitchens is his historical significance. For Villa, his departure was another step towards failure. For the English game as a whole, he pioneered where many would follow. His achievements deserve to be recognised.

PLATT, David

Position: Attacking midfield.
Born: Oldham, 10 June 1966
Career: South Chadderton Comprehensive School (Oldham), Boundary Park Juniors, Chadderton (amateur), Manchester United, (apprentice, June 1982, professional, July 1984), Crewe Alexandra (free, February 1985), ASTON VILLA (£200,000, February 1988), Bari/Italy (£5.5 million, July 1991), Juventus, Italy (£6.5 million, June 1992), Sampdoria, Italy (£5.25 million, August 1993), Arsenal (£4.75 million, July 1995), Sampdoria, Italy (free transfer, player/coach/manager, August 1995–November 1998), Nottingham Forest (player-manager, August 1999: retired July 2001), England Under-21 coach/manager (2001–May 2004), Manchester City (first-team coach, 1 July 2010)

England:
Caps: 62, Won: 29, Lost: 9, Drawn: 24, Goals: 27
With the Villa he won 22 caps. He won the rest of his caps (40) playing with Bari, Juventus and Arsenal – the living proof that playing abroad no longer hindered an England career. It was his Villa career made his reputation.

Early Years
There are two classic types of successful international player at Aston Villa – the

talented player who is identified as skilful from the earliest days – like Billy Walker or Gordon Cowans – or the apparent journeyman player whose potential is uncertain but develops into a top-quality player by personal effort and good coaching, like Gerry Hitchens. David Platt is the finest example of the second type of player.

That he had talent was obvious, and Manchester United took him on as a teenager. But they then let him go, believing his potential was too problematic to gamble on. United then watched as Crewe's Dario Gradi honed his talent in the Fourth Division and sold him on to Villa, then in the Second Division, who took him into the old First Division and made him an international player of the highest class under the eagle eye of manager Graham Taylor.

Though David Platt was football daft as a youngster, he was never an outstanding schoolboy footballer. He had technical weaknesses, notably a failure to use his left foot. However, he acquired a strong work ethic particularly from his father, a key influence in his life. His father and elder brother trained him by making him use just his left foot to kick the ball, something he remains eternally grateful for. His father remained on the scene even after Platt moved in with his mother on their divorce, when he was 15, and it is clear good relations with his parents proved crucial to his well balanced, hard working nature.

He played on the wings for his school team to minimise physical challenges. At his comprehensive he played for the school, but equally important was his time with Boundary Park Juniors. Unlike school, this had professional training routines and Platt began to develop strength and tactical awareness. Platt played for Olham Town Team at schoolboy level, but there he got stuck. He played for the school, Chadderton amateurs and Boundary Park Juniors – three games every weekend – but it went no further.

No club was interested in him when he left school. This experience sowed a seed of doubt in his mind, and he was not fully convinced of his ability until he reached the very top. His career went through an odd pattern of long periods when nothing much happened, then a rapid step up to another level.

His first experience of this was getting to Manchester United as a trainee. His three games a weekend paid off, he was spotted and asked to join the Youth Training Scheme as an apprentice. Yet Platt was a very small fish in a very big pond. Although he soon got a year's contract as a professional, he was at this time playing as a forward, and United had six in line before him. He was loaned

out to Crewe Alexandra, and their excellent manager, Dario Gradi, saw his potential as an attacking midfielder. He asked to sign Platt full time. Ron Atkinson, the United manager, agreed, but in letting Platt go said to him 'I always liked you in practice matches against the first team because you worked hard and caused them problems. Never stop working hard and remember this conversation when you win your first England cap'. (*Autobiography* p.31). A curious remark to make to a player you are letting go.

Ron Atkinson later told the journalist Leon Hickman 'I always had a feeling he was going to make it. There was something about him. I don't make too many mistakes, but he was one'. But Platt often did not get even a Central League game. At 18, he needed regular football, which Crewe could offer him. Stepping into a Fourth Division side was not so much a step down, as the chance to be coached and play regularly after he moved to Crewe in February 1985.

Dario Gradi turned Platt from a forward who could operate in midfield to a midfield attacker, exploiting Platt's natural athleticism to good effect. Clubs started making offers, rising to £150,00 from Hibs and Villa. Villa were the ideal club, a Second Division club recovering from relegation under Graham Taylor. However, Gradi wanted £200,000 for the 22-year-old, which seemed excessive. Platt writes in his autobiography 'My immediate reaction was that no-one would pay that. I had scored 19 goals in 21 games for Crewe that season but they were in the fourth division. I wasn't worth that much'. (p.49)

What he did not know was that Graham Taylor had driven to see Crewe play Newport on a wet and windy night before 1,200 people and saw Platt dribble from the halfway line and chip just over the bar. Taylor was convinced Platt was a skilled and committed footballer and was prepared to pay the extra £50,000. On 28 January 1988 Platt signed for Villa.

The Villa Experience

Platt signed a three-and-a-half-year contract, and the first half season was a roller coaster with Villa only getting promotion on the last day of the season. A week later Platt was called up for the England Under-21 side alongside Paul Gascoigne. Gazza's skill and ebullient personality was a boon for Platt, since it took the media spotlight away from him and allowed him to develop – a role Gazza unwittingly played throughout their England careers. Platt realised he did not have Gazza's phenomenal skill. What he took a long time to understand was that he had qualities which were far more useful to a side, particularly consistency. As an Italian journalist told Leon Hickman after the 1990 World Cup: 'You see, while your papers are talking about Gazza this and Gazza that, the one who impressed us was Platt. He can play and score goals. That makes him very valuable'. (Hickman, p.174)

But Italian interest was for the future. Going into the First Division, Platt had doubts. He later wrote 'I wondered if it was all too much for me, whether playing against top quality professional players week in and week out was beyond my capabilities'. (*Autobiography*, p.61). However, in a poor season for Villa, it was the other players who looked out of their depth as Villa survived the 1988–89 season only fourth from bottom. Taylor had to make major changes, but David Platt was never under threat. Indeed, in the formation Taylor then adopted – three central defenders, four in midfield, two wingers (Daley and Ormondroyd on the wings, and only Ian Olney as out-and-out striker) – the combination of Platt and Gordon Cowans, now returned from Italy, was vital.

Platt commented of his debt to Cowans and to his father for making him work on his weak foot, 'Gordon is the best footballer I have ever played alongside...My left foot will never be as good as Gordon Cowans, but I am grateful to my father. I am sure I would have been one footed otherwise'. (Hickman, p.180). On the pitch the right sided Platt and the left sided Cowans complemented each other. Cowans and Platt also had the same attitude to their profession, both had the work ethic. Just as Platt had worked with his father and brother on improving skills, Platt stayed late with Cowans and assistant manager John Ward to practise Platt's finishing skills. (Hickman, p.192). Like all great players, Cowans and Platt knew the value of practice and hard work on the training ground.

The work paid off. 1989–90 was a superb year for Graham Taylor's side. Going into the second half of the season they topped the table, and Platt's form earned him a new contract. Negotiations were complicated, but finally the details were completed. Platt celebrated with two goals in a 6–2 rout of Everton, and Graham Taylor rewarded the team with a Monday off. Platt went to see a friend, only to get a call from his girlfriend's mother. Villa Park were desperate to speak to him, please would he ring the club. Platt expected a hitch with the contract. He was stunned to hear that Bobby Robson had called him into the England squad.

Robson made him substitute for a game against Italy, on 15 November 1989, sending him on for Peter Beardsley in the last 13 minutes. With England having qualified for the 1990 World Cup, Robson was assessing the final few places in his squad. Platt was on the fringe, normally as a subtitute. He was given a full match against Brazil in March 1990, but was back as substitute in May. A week later he failed to start at all, in June he made another substitute appearance against Tunisia.

He was chosen for the final squad as he had supporters in the camp, notably assistant manager Don Howe who commented on the choice of

Gascoigne and Platt in midfield that 'Platt hadn't got the skills and grace, but was reliable and would get in the box, then get back in position. Gazza had all the flair and imagination, but would go missing. On League form, I was more impressed with Platt' (*England Expects*, James Corbett, p.404). Howe was right, but once inside the box, Platt could also score. Overall, his phenomenal contribution to the Villa's season was recognised when the PFA voted him Player of the Year, one of only three Villa players ever to get the award – the others being Andy Gray and Paul McGrath. Robson chose both Platt and Gascoigne.

But Platt was still on the margins, saying 'I was just a squad player. I had no illusions whatever about being anything else, and to be honest, given the quality of the company I was in, I didn't expect to be on the bench for any of our games'. (*Autobiography*, p.76) He was on the bench, but he was indeed a squad player. For the first game in Italy he did not play at all. But life as a super sub was about to end with a super goal.

His eighth cap was against Belgium on 21 June 1990, a game England had to win to go beyond the qualifying round. It was a 0–0 draw when he was sent on, substituting for Steve McMahon on 71 minutes. The game went into extra-time and as time ran out was heading for penalties. Then, with a minute to go, England got a free -kick 50 yards out. This was the last attack of the match. Platt went on the end of the Belgian wall as Gascoigne floated the free kick over the wall. As it dropped, Platt peeled off the wall, pivoted, and hit the ball as sweet as a nut beyond the Belgian goalkeeper. England were through, and David Platt was ecstatic and was a national hero.

Never again did Robson choose him as substitute. He scored against Cameroon, and again in the Play-off for third place against Italy. The Italians noticed that he had come of age in footballing terms. While Gascoigne took the headlines, Platt was able to get on with his job unhindered. He came back to England an established international.

With Villa having finished second the previous season, fans hoped that the club would push on for the Championship. But Bobby Robson quit the England job, and to the detriment of Aston Villa Graham Taylor was chosen as his successor. Doug Ellis appointed Dr Jo Venglos as manager, a pioneering experiment with a foreign manager which did not work. The season after the World Cup was a horrible one for Villa, who dropped from second to 17th, and understandably David Platt looked elsewhere to further his career.

Taylor, of course, maintained the new Robson policy of making Platt a first-choice England player. He missed only one of Taylor's first 12 games, after which he was no longer a Villa player. Curiously, for his third match as manager. Taylor chose to recall Gordon Cowans. If he hoped to recreate the Villa partnership, it did not work. Cowans never played for England again, but Platt went on to win 62 caps.

Only 22 of these were with Aston Villa. In the summer of 1992 Platt followed Gordon Cowans to Bari in Italy, for a British transfer record of £5.5 million. His career soared, and he moved on to Juventus and Sampdoria, and then back to England again with Arsenal. He became England captain, the pinnacle of a highly successful career. It reflected great credit on both the player and Villa under Graham Taylor, who took a Fourth Division footballer and trained him into a first-class one.

The ultimate credit lies with Platt himself. Few players have ever been rejected by a major club, dropped into the Fourth Divison (now League Two), and rebuilt their career to reach the heights. That his career was overshadowed by Paul Gascoigne was a blessing in disguise, but there is no doubt who proved the more successful, on and off the pitch.

WALKER, Billy

Position: Inside-forward
Born: Wednesbury, 29 October 1897
Died: Sheffield, 28 November 1964
Career: Walsall Boys, Hednesford Town, Wednesbury Old Athletic, Wednesbury Old Park, Darlaston, ASTON VILLA (December 1914 amateur, professional June 1920–November 1933 when he retired), Sheffield Wednesday (manager, December 1933–November 1937), Chelmsford City (Manager January–October 1938), Nottingham Forest (manager, March 1939–July 1960). Played eight games for Forest during World War Two.

England
Caps: 18, Won: 9, Lost: 4, Drawn: 5, Goals: 9

Billy Walker was the greatest Villa player of the 1920s, and one of the very few to captain both Villa and England. He only ever played professionally for the

Villa, signing amateur forms at Christmas 1914 when 17, during the wartime soccer break, becoming a professional in 1920. He was converted from centre-forward to inside-forward, was excellent at playing with attacking wingers. He notably partnered centre-forward Pongo Waring when he set the record for goals scored in the goal glut season of 1930–31. Villa alas just failed just to win the Championship despite scoring one goal more than champions Arsenal.

His scoring record was phenomenal: he scored 244 goals in 531 League and FA Cup appearances, overtaking Harry Hampton's total of 242 by two – the record of 244 still the best total by a Villa player. 'Appy 'Arry in fact scored one more League goal – 215 to Walker's 214 – but Walker scored 30 in taking part in a record number of FA Cup ties. There were, of course, no other competitions at the time, so comparisons are difficult to make: and the appearance records of Charlie Aitken and Gordon Cowans in overtaking Walker are outstanding.in their own right. But Walker not only had fewer competitions to appear in but substitutions were not allowed in Walker's day, appearances lasted for the full 90 minutes unless seriously injured. It was a tougher game. (Stats from autobiography p.9)

Walker's goal record is more impressive when it is noted that, unlike Harry Hampton, he was an inside-forward not a centre-forward – though Hampton's career was cut short by the war. But Walker scored 11 hat-tricks, nine in the First Division (he only ever played in the First Division), and two in the FA Cup. He was a regular penalty taker, and one of the very few players in history to have scored a hat-trick of penalties, three in one game, doing so against Bradford City in November 1921. He played with Arthur Dorrell in the mid 1920s on the left wing, and reached double figures in the scoring charts in every season 1919–20 to 1930–31, his best record being in the 1920–21, when he scored 32 goals in 42 appearances. He then partnered the young Eric Houghton when Dorrell retired.

His scoring record for England, one in every two games, is more than respectable. Goalscoring is, of course, what a forward is paid to do, but what made Walker arguably a greater player than Hampton at a time when the game was still sufficiently unchanged to make a comparison fair, is that he was a much better all-round player. Hampton appears to have relied on aggression to a large extent, barging the goalkeeper into the net, which was allowed in the pre-television days, but Walker does not appear to have done so. He was noted as a tactician, though there is little evidence remaining on how he played. He was Villa captain for six seasons, 1926–32.

He was able to play as goalkeeper in an emergency, doing so for England against France in Paris in 1925 when Fred Fox was injured, playing in the second half and aiding a victory by 3–2. Above all, Walker could read the game and the players around him – as his career in management showed – one of the few Villa players who had real leadership potential. He was a good man for a crisis. And for the crucial match against Austria in 1932, then the best side in Europe, it is remarkable he was called back after five years in the wilderness and made captain. It was an emergency, and the Villa selectors turned to a man they knew would rise to the occasion. He did, and England won a thriller 4–3. But he never played for England again.

The Making of a Great Player

Two types of footballer emerge from the records – the naturally talented and the player coached to greatness. Walker was the first type. He knew while playing schoolboy football he had the talent to succeed, yet his parents did everything to keep him from taking up a football career. He was academically bright and they wanted a career in business or the professions for him. Walker's father was a professional for Wolverhampton Wanderers and knew the career to be short, insecure and after the maximum wage was brought in, poorly paid.

George Walker had limited talent – his son describes him as a 'clogger' full-back – so never won honours. His only claim to fame was that after being seriously injured tripping on a bad pitch at Swindon in 1907 he was the first player to claim for lost wages under the Workman's Compensation Act. (*Autobiography*, p.19, also article in *Villa News & Record*, 1 September 1909, which says Walker was not the only appellant).

Walker's parents had other reasons to deter their son from football. He was a sickly child, prone to colds and after playing football in the rain he caught a chill which turned into tuberculosis. He spent three months in a sanatorium and had over 100 injections before the disease cleared from his left lung (*Autobiography*, pp.11–12). Worse, he contracted rickets, the vitamin deficiency disease which prevents bone developing properly. His legs would collapse underneath him without warning. Luckily, from age 10 onward the disease cleared up, but he was left with deformed knees, almost double jointed, which became a gift to cartoonists while he played. (*Autobiography*, pp.20–21).

However, as a schoolboy he clearly had the talent to succeed and at 13, he made a crucial choice when coming up to the exam for the grammar school – the school leaving age then was 14 – but working-class children could win a scholarship. Both he and his sister were clever enough to pass the exam, which his sister did, but Walker realised that passing meant he would not be able to play school football. He had set a record of 80 goals in 25 games for Kings Hill School in the Walsall Schools League. Aware of his talent, he deliberately failed the exam, but then left school at 14 to work in a factory. As the title of his

autobiography states, he had football in the blood. His father told him football was 'hard work, hard knocks, hard criticism, no fortune, few good friends – that's football. Try farming, go to sea, drive a bus. Anything but the College of Kicks' (*Autobiography*, p.19).

Walker ignored the advice, but prospects were not good. Wolves took no interest in him, but both Birmingham and Villa invited him to play in occasional wartime games. His chances looked slim, for he was only 9st 5lb and lacked physical strength. The amy examined him four times as a potential recruit, but rejected him on medical grounds. But when the war ended and football restarted he was aged nearly 22, and Walker had gained the physical strength allied with natural talent to make an impact on the game. Talent is never enough without determination, and he had it in bucketloads.

Walker Starts His Villa Career

Walker was at this point a centre-forward, a problem position as Harry Hampson was coming to the end of his career. Six forwards were tried before he was given the nod in an FA Cup tie against Queen's Park Rangers on 10 January 1920. He scored both the goals and Villa had found the replacement for 'Appy 'Arry. A week later he made the first of 478 League appearances, all in the First Division and all for Villa.

Once in the team he could not be shifted, and in every season from 1919–20 to 1930–31 Billy Walker achieved a double-figure tally of goals scored, with 31 in 1920–21. He terrified defences, with a four timer against Arsenal in 1920. The FA Cup victory that year should have been the start of the trophies, but Villa were in decline. The problem was in defence, not the forward line and no one could blame Walker, who was outstanding. The 1921 *Villa News* quoted a report that Villa was still a football university, but in fact it would be 50 years until that was true again.

When the great football journalist and international Charles Buchan looked back at the first half of the century in his autobiography, Buchan selected two great sides from the players he saw before and after the change in the offside rule in 1925. Billy Walker was the only Villa player to make the cut in the post-1925 selection. The team was Hibbs (Birmingham), Cooper (Derby), Hapgood (Arsenal), Edwards (Leeds), Cullis (Wolves), Weaver (Newcastle) Matthews (Stoke), Kelly (Burnley), Dean (Everton), Walker (Villa), Dimmock (Spurs). To be named in the same forward line as Stanley Matthews and Dixie Dean was no mean feat. The IFHHS international survey also awarded high praise. And for fans who saw him in the 1920s and 1930s, like my father and grandfather, Billy Walker was a player to savour.

Villa News & Record, 19 February 1921, p.348

'What we have worried over latterly has been his seemingly lost art of getting goals. But...the following extracts from a "personal" sketch in a London contemporary (sic) will be of interest. Walker has already achieved a prominent place among the centre-forwards of the day. With a keen nose for an opening, he is fast and clever and has a rasping shot in either foot. His height enables him to be deadly with the "third foot". At present he is a shade slow in recovery, perhaps, but that is a fault that education and experience will mend, and Walker is fortunate enough to be an undergraduate in one of the best Soccer Universities in the world – the Aston Villa Football Club.'

The IFFHS comments: 'A great strategist able to find his team mates in the best position on the pitch. He was one of the most popular British players in the 1920s'. p.94

Eye-witness account in 1960:

'But to me, whose schoolboy hero he was, Billy Walker will always be a Villa man, irrespective of his associations and successes at Sheffield and Nottingham...Not since Hampton's heyday had a Villa crowd idolised a player as they did Walker. Even "Pongo" Waring, their "darling" of the mid-thirties, never achieved quite the same popularity.'

'Walker ranks as the third member in the distinguished trio of Aston Villa's great inside-forwards, the other two clearly being John Devey and Joe Bache. He played a prominent part in Villa's affairs over a period of 13 years. The young Walker eventually took over the "master" role vacated by Joe Bache in the Villa attack, and not only did he "make" two successive Villa left wingers into internationals, Arthur Dorrell and Eric Houghton, but partnered each of them in turn for England.' Peter Morris, *Aston Villa*, 1962, pp.114–115

Villa Internationals

AGBONLAHOR, Gabriel Imuetinyan (Gabby)

Position: Striker

Born: Erdington, Birmingham, 13 October 1986

Career: Great Barr Falcons; ASTON VILLA (academy 1994–2005); Sheffield Wednesday (loan 2005); Watford (loan 2005); ASTON VILLA (2005–present)

England

Caps: 3, Won: 2, Lost: 1, Drawn: 0, Goals: 0

Gabriel Agbonlahor, English by nationality but initially qualified for Nigeria and Scotland by parentage, came through the Villa academy system where he was a highly successful striker, mainly at centre-forward. Only a few players ever rise from playing in the Academy to become successful in the Premiership: Agbonlahor became a fixture in the side while only 20 – he played in every Premiership game in the 2006–07 season though only 19 when the season started – and broke through at international level under Fabio Capello.

Agbonlahor began his professional career in the 2005–06 season with 10 games on loan, two for Watford and eight for Sheffield Wednesday, without scoring. He was 19 when an crisis forced then manager David O'Leary to give him a Premiership run which was not planned. On 18 March 2006 he was called on as substitute for the last 20 minutes of a dreadful team performance at Goodison Park which the Villa were well on the way to losing 4–1. The only bright spot was an excellent goal by Agbonlahor, who ran at the defence from midfield, and coolly shot with power and precision. It was clear he was fast, but more impressive from my viewpoint was that he shot with very little backlift, and the Everton goalie hardly moved.

Neverthless, while he played another eight games that season he did not score again. It was the next season, 2006–07, when he really made his mark by playing in every Premiership game under new manager Martin O'Neill. For a player only just 20 this was a big ask. He scored nine goals that season in the Premiership plus a winner in the League Cup. Moreover, he showed a talent for scoring against the then Big Four (Manchester United, Chelsea, Arsenal and Liverpool) that would

become a personal trait, scoring against Chelsea in a 1–1 draw on 30 September 1986 – when he was not yet 20. He followed that up by scoring his first goal against Liverpool a month later, and Manchester United on 13 January 2007.

He is a player who thrives on pressure, and the pressure on a young player who became a fixture very quickly has been massive. He has coped well. He played 37 Premiership games in the next (2007–08) season plus two League Cup games and an FA Cup appearance. He totalled 11 goals, all in the Premiership, scoring again against Manchester United in a 4–1 defeat and the winner in the Birmingham-Villa derby in November, in the 86th minute. Sixty seconds earlier he had cleared off the line, combining of successful defensive duties and the winning goal to show there is more to his game than mere pace.

Such a good season led to high expectations, but the 2008–09 season marked time. In part this was because he scored a so called 'perfect' hat-trick – header and shots with both feet – in the first Premiership home game, against Manchester City, then only scored eight more goals all season – though he played 50 games in total, still only 22! The hat-trick was scored in seven minutes, making it the second-fastest in Premiership history. The relative lack of goals after that during the season led to unjustified crowd irritation at Villa Park.

By the end of the 2009–10 season, Gabby Agbonlahor had more games for the Villa than any other player under Martin O'Neill. He was the only player to have survived from the years before O'Neill with 172 starts, 13 substitute appearances and 51 goals. Only Stilian Petrov, O'Neill's first signing, (152+7) and Ashley Young (147+3) rivalled him for appearances in the O'Neill era.

His first cap followed a victory against Arsenal at the Emirates, in which the record books noted that he scored, finally scoring against Arsenal to make a full bag of goals against the Big Four. What the record books do not show is that the second goal, scored by Gael Clichy of Arsenal, came about because Clichy tried to pass back to his goalkeeper with Agbonlahor coming up at speed in the inside-right channel, panicked and hit the ball past his own goalkeeper. As with Heskey, the number of goals scored is not the only part of his game. He terrifies opposition defenders when playing through the middle. John Terry of England and Chelsea said 'He is a nightmare to play against'.

England

He was qualified by his parentage to play for Nigeria and Scotland as well as England, and on 20 September 2006 he had been pencilled in for the Nigerian Under-20 team, but turned down the chance. A week later he received his first call up for the Under-21 team and made his first appearance at Under-21 level on 6 October 2006, a week short of his 20th birthday. He was omitted from the Under-21 on 30 September 2007, after missing the Under-21 training camp in Spain. He had just played his first full season under Martin O'Neill, and the suspension was only temporary. By September 2007 he was back in the Under-21 side.

After he had played 16 games for the Under-21 side between 2006 and 2009, scoring five goals, he was well known to the England managership. In February 2008 he was called up by Capello. He could not play due to injury, but was an unused substitute in England matches in May–June 2008. Capello picked him for his first cap on 19 November 2008. He played for 76 minutes in his first game, and had a goal disallowed, before being replaced by Ashley Young. John Terry, then England captain, made the remark already quoted after the match. For his second match on 11 February 2009 he played for 75 minutes before being substituted for Carlton Cole.

When, on 14 October 2009 Capello awarded him his third cap against Belarus, this was a perfect birthday present – he was 23 the previous day. It was his first competitive match for England, and he managed an assist before being replaced by Carlton Cole in the 66th minute. Agbonlahor has yet to score for the full England team. The Belarus game was the 162nd game he had played at senior level: a remarkable testimony to his fitness, skill, fine temperament and excellent work ethic. This was the last cap he has won so far, but he was called into the squad for the Denmark friendly on 9 February 2011. Alas he had to withdraw due to family matters.

Agbonlahor is a flexible, athletic modern striker and has so far showed himself able to fulfil his considerable potential. He has not yet reached the limit of what he is capable of. In January 2011 he signed four-and-a-half-year contract, and said he sees no way of moving from Villa Park. His 200th appearance was in the Sunderland game 5 January 2011. He is a real local hero and in February 2011 visited local youth club Boldmere Falcons to present a cheque for £464,129 from the Football Foundation to develop a 3G pitch and state of the art pavilion. He may yet qualify for the 300 club.

ALLEN, Albert

Position: Forward

Born: Aston, Birmingham, 7 April 1867

Died: Birmingham, 13 October 1899
Career: St Phillip's FC, Aston; ASTON VILLA (August 1884–May 1891).

England

Caps: 1, Won: 1, Lost: 0, Drawn: 0, Goals: 3

Albert Allen is one of the 'lost' players of Aston Villa in two ways – he was involved too early in the club's career to have proper records in the club archive, as the club had no real record in its early years, and played too few games at either club or international level to attract the interest of journalists who might have written articles to flesh out the bare statistics with useful information. Allen played in the years before and after the Football League was set up in the 1888–89 season, and with only 12 teams in the League for the three seasons he competed he had very limited chances to play for the club. This may account for his playing record. He started playing for the Villa aged only 17, which meant he could not play many games in his early years. Officially he only played 56 games; however, in this limited number of games he scored 33 times, notching Villa's first-ever Football League hat-trick against Notts County in September 1888.

Allen did not have an England career – one game is not a career – but it is surprising that, given the fact that he scored a hat-trick in the game against Ireland in March 1888, he never played again. His lack of further caps and limited number of games for the Villa are puzzling. He retired through injury at the end of the 1890–91 season, aged only 24, and died very young, at just 32, so perhaps there was a physical weakness which limited his prospects.

Villa News 1, 1 September 1906
A light but most effective wing player, with a good turn of speed. Lack of weight and size did not affect his pluck. Dribbled like an artist and shot with force and good aim. Always did well in big games, and was seen to special advantage in his international. A modest, unassuming player whom it was a pleasure to meet.

ATHERSMITH, Charlie

Position: Outside-right

Born: Bloxwich, Staffordshire, 10 May 1872

Died: Shifnal, 18 September 1910

See Pantheon section for full details.

BACHE, Joseph

Position: Forward, normally inside-left

Born: Stourbridge, 8 February 1880

Died: 10 November 1960

Career: Stourbridge (July 1897); ASTON VILLA, professional (December 1900); Mid Rhondda, player-manager (August 1919); Grimsby Town, player-coach (August 1920); SG Rot-Weiss, Frankfurt, coach-trainer (May 1921); Mannheim FC, player (October 1924); ASTON VILLA, reserve-team coach (1926–27); Mannheim, coach (1928); SG Rot-Weiss, coach (1929).

After his retirement Bache returned to live in Birmingham.

England

Caps: 7, Won: 4, Lost: 0, Drawn: 3, Goals: 4

Of the many outstanding characters in this book, three stand out as managers as well as players, Joe Bache (pronounced 'Baishe'), Eric Houghton and Billy Walker, the last two being FA Cup-winners as managers.

Houghton and Walker are legends, but Bache is almost totally forgotten, despite an outstanding record which reached the heights at international level. How many now recall his record in succeeding Howard Spencer as captain from the 1908–09 season and leading the club to League and Cup glory in 1910 and 1913, adding a second Cup medal to the one he had won in 1905?

What made Bache unique, however, was that he was one of the pioneers of the international game, playing and managing in Germany after World War One at a time when English coaches were wanted abroad – unlike today. He deserves more recognition for his record of 474 first-team games and 184 goals and his contribution to the game for England and on the Continent.

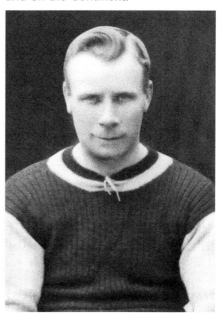

He was not always an unknown figure. A few years after he retired the *Villa News & Record* commented that 'many Villa spectators will remember Joe Bache with a good deal of admiration...he was a great favourite with the crowd, especially when he started getting the opposing defence in a tangle, and passing to a clubmate in a favourable position.' (*Villa News & Record,* 23 February 1924). The programme had commented at the time of the 1913 Cup Final, 'He does with skill what others do with speed...he seems to hand rather than kick the ball to his inside colleagues.' In 1906 the programme had not been so complimentary, but seven years later his qualities were better appreciated. Normally played at inside-left, he was moved to outside-left at the end of his career, which was odd since this meant more distance to cover. His left-wing partnership with Albert Hall was legendary, but they were criticised for forgetting the other three forwards at times. He then formed another brilliant partnership with Clem Stephenson, who was a lost player in another way.

As an international player his record was excellent but intermittent – he never became a first-choice player. He has the proud record of never playing in a losing England side. While his seven caps were awarded from eight years 1903 to 1911, suggesting that he tended to be brought in as a stopgap, he never let England down. He scored in each of his first four international games, giving England the lead against Wales after 12 minutes on his debut. After these games, in 1903, 1904 and 1905, he was not called up again till 1907 and then again in 1910 and 1911 – hardly the regular pattern to bring out the best in a player.

After the war his career as a coach was remarkable as this meant overcoming the language barrier, although his family was of German origin. When he returned and was employed by the Villa, he did not establish himself on the backroom staff, which may have been another mistake by a club starting to slip from the highest standards. Sadly, Bache was too easily forgotten.

Villa News & Record 1, 1 September 1906
'Gained his honours (during a period not too prolific of star performers) after a series of exceptionally clever displays in club matches for Aston Villa...Mars much of his otherwise effective play by his impetuosity in endeavouring to do too much in the zone of the backs. On his day a dangerous shot, but apt to be erratic, as well as a trifle selfish. A good-tempered, brainy player.'

Villa News & Record, 23 April 1913, p548:

'A veteran with the speed of a lad…He always bears out the truth of the football axiom that it is three to one on the man with the ball. He does by skill what others do by speed when nothing will suffice…He seems to hand rather than kick the ball to his inside colleagues. Still a great player.'

BARRETT, Earl Delliser

Position: Defender
Born: Rochdale, 28 April 1967
Career: Manchester City, juniors (1983), professional (April 1985); Chester City, on loan (March 1986); Oldham Athletic (November 1987); ASTON VILLA, £1.7 million (February 1992); Everton, £1.7 million (January 1995); Sheffield United, on loan (January 1998); Sheffield Wednesday (February 1998–July 1999).

England

Caps: 3, Won: 1, Lost: 1, Drawn 1

Earl Barrett was signed by Ron Atkinson during his first season as Villa manager (1991–92) to shore up the right side of Villa's defence. Although Big Ron is normally seen as an attack-minded manager, he was well aware that no side ever wins if they cannot defend. His priority on arriving at Villa was a strike forward, and he broke Villa's transfer record in signing Dalian Atkinson for £1.6 million in an eye-catching signing. He identified defensive weaknesses, however, and in February 1992 broke the record a second time to sign Earl Barrett to play at right-back. With Steve Staunton signed at left-back for £1.1 million, Atkinson had spent serious money on full-backs who could play down the wings and support the attackers.

Earl Barrett had already won one England cap on 3 June 1991 in a friendly in New Zealand. By coming to Villa aged 24 and reaching his prime, he aimed to establish himself on a bigger stage than Oldham, where he had made his name and won his first cap. He had come to prominence in Oldham's Second Division Championship season 1990–91, winning a Championship medal, and was widely anticipated to go on to higher things. Indeed, after establishing himself at Villa in the 1991–92 season he had an excellent two seasons from 1992–94. Villa peaked in 1992–93, though, coming second to Manchester United in the League but failing to push on the next season. While United strode to another title in 1993–94 with even more points, Villa fell back to 10th. There were growing tensions between manager Atkinson and chair Doug Ellis, which would lead eventually to Atkinson being sacked and replaced by Brian Little.

During the positive early period Barrett won the second and third of his England caps and the League Cup with the Villa. His England career

peaked in June 1993 with caps against Brazil – a 1–1 draw – and Germany with a 2–1 defeat, and he never played for England again. He was called up by manager Graham Taylor on the strength of his Villa form for a friendly tournament in the USA, as Taylor sought players who could salvage England's failing 1994 World Cup bid. England had already lost to the USA when Barrett came in, and while the England performance was creditable they failed to defeat major sides Germany and Brazil. The impression is that the England management were looking for a left-sided defender, but Barrett did not answer Taylor's requirements.

His Villa career culminated in the League Cup victory over Manchester United in 1994. Villa went into the match as clear underdogs, but a 4–5–1 formation stifled United's attackers and Barrett played a major role in keeping United down to one goal late in the game. This enabled Villa's forwards to counter attack to secure a famous victory. Villa's 10th place was a big disappointment, however, and with his England career going nowhere Barrett was transferred to Everton in January 1995. It was an odd decision – Everton were 17th in 1994 and would finish only 15th in 1995 and, while they were to win the FA Cup in 1995, they were not a great side. Villa finished 18th in a 22-club League, though, and it was clear that Big Ron had taken the club as far as he could. Barrett did not revive his England career by moving, but he certainly made a wise decision in leaving a club in decline.

BARRY, Gareth

Position: Midfield
Born: Hastings, 23 February 1981
Career: Brighton (associate schoolboy forms); ASTON VILLA (apprentice, June 1997, professional, 27 February 1998); transferred to Manchester City 2 June 2009.

England
Caps: ongoing; with Villa, total is 29

Barry is an excellent footballer, and could have been a Villa Park legend, but chose other priorities. This is a pity, for the achievements he recorded while a Villa player were considerable. Signed from Brighton in 1997 as an apprentice along with Michael Standing, he was an outstanding talent from the start. After only eight months as an apprentice he was signed as a professional, often playing in midfield though he initially regarded himself as a left back. He made his senior debut as substitute in the last but one match of the 1997–98 season, and his full debut in the last match of that season, against Arsenal.

He quickly became a fixture in the team, and on 28 October 2007 he became the youngest player to date to complete 300 Premiership games, overtaking Frank Lampard at the age of 26 years and 247 days. Barry was made captain and his rise continued to be meteoric, converting from being a defender to becoming a most effective attacking midfield player.

Barry represented England at Youth, Under-21 and full levels, getting his first cap against Ukraine on 31 May 2000, aged just 19. However after six caps in 2000, his progress stalled. He gained another two in 2003, but no more till the start of the Martin O'Neill regime. Sven-Goran Eriksson decided he did not fit in but after the departure of Eriksson in 2007 he became a regular in the England side. The new manager Steve McLaren brought him on as sub on 7 February 2007. Fabio Capello continued to select him and he has the unusual record of having played under five different England managers. He won 29 caps while at Villa but announced he wished to be transferred – to a club with a chance of experiencing Champion's League football, or so it was said.

Villa became involved in a bitter dispute with Liverpool in the summer of 2008 following their bid to sign Barry, with a rumour that he wished to play with long-time associate Steven Gerrard. It was therefore surprising when Barry eventually signed in June 2009 for Manchester City, a club which was not in the Champion's League, but who had been taken over by oil billionaires. Since his move to Manchester, Barry has continued to be picked for the England team.

The desire to win European glory is wholly understandable, and no serious supporter blames Barry for wanting this. The positive reception to Olaf Mellberg when he transferred to Juventus to compete in Europe shows that Villa fans do see the challenges facing top players. Barry is one of four Villa players to have captained England while at Villa Park. He has shown that an England career can be built at Villa Park.

BARSON, Frank

Position: Centre-half
Born: Grimesthorpe, Sheffield, 10 April 1891
Died: Winson Green, Birmingham, 13 September 1968
Career: Albion FC, Sheffield; Cammell Laird FC, Sheffield; Barnsley (August 1911); ASTON VILLA, £2,850 (October 1919); Manchester United (August 1922); Watford (May 1928); Hartlepools United, player-coach (May 1929); Wigan Borough, amateur (October 1929), then professional again (July 1930); Rhyl Athletic, player-manager (June 1931); Stourbridge, manager (July–August

1930); ASTON VILLA, youth-team coach (August 1935), senior coach and head trainer (October 1935); Swansea Town, trainer (July 1947–February 1954) Lye Town, trainer (July 1954–April 1956).

Barson retired from football on his 65th birthday.

England

Caps: 1, Won: 0, Lost: 1, Drawn: 0

Of all the players in this book, Frank Barson is the greatest underachiever, spoiling his career by overly aggressive behaviour. He only won one cap, though there is no doubt about his ability – or the notoriety caused by his disciplinary record. When Villa broke their transfer record to buy him from Barnsley in October 1919, aged 28, he still had the best years of a war-disrupted career ahead of him and enormous potential, but he won only one cap, plus an FA Cup-winners' medal with Villa, in 1920. By August 1922 he was transferred to Manchester United for another large sum, £5,000, apparently because, like Hardy and Clem Stephenson, he would not move home, claiming he would 'never move to Brummagem'. There was more to his career than mere cussedness, though. Unlike Hardy and Stephenson, he was a character as much feared as respected.

In an age of stopper centre-halves, Barson stood out for aggressiveness. He was a clogger of a defender. The clogger, a player who frequently fouls when tackling, does not exist today, physical contact being limited and defenders required to distribute the ball, not simply boot it away. While 'hacking' – kicking another player – was outlawed when soccer was created, the shoulder charge and using sheer muscle to stop the other player playing was allowed till the 1980s. Despite referees allowing more physical contact than today, Barson consistently went too far. He was sent off at least 12 times, twice while playing for Villa, and served a year of suspensions. On one occasion while playing for Manchester United, he served six weeks for allegedly knocking another player unconscious. At Watford he served a six-month suspension for a similar offence. His aggressiveness was legendary. His transfer to Villa, for a record fee, was after a row with the Barnsley committee, and he then fell out with the Villa committee.

Such a man was a high-risk character, too abrasive to be picked more than once for England due to his brushes with authority. Page 439 in the 2 April 1921 edition of the *Villa News* noted that two members of the international selection committee had attended the Villa versus Chelsea semi-final that year and had praised Barson, Billy Walker and Richard York. None were picked for the next international, though Charlie Wallace won his last cap. Walker and York were capped for England in subsequent years, however. Barson never got another cap, no matter how well he played.

He was transferred to Manchester United in August 1922 after the Reds

had been relegated from Division One. No First Division club wanted to pay a big fee for him. Barson played at the top until 1928, when he was 37, and after a career in the lower divisions returned to Villa in 1935 as head trainer for the best part of 12 years.

Villa fans had never lost their affection for Barson. Billy Walker, an intelligent and perceptive man, looked beyond the thuggish image and saw Barson as a hard man but not dirty: a man within the Villa tradition. Jimmy Hogan employed him in the 1930s to run the youth team, Hogan being a good judge of character as well as ability, and Rinder singled him out for praise at the July 1938 AGM (*Villa News* p.506). He never again left Birmingham and died in Winson Green aged 77. Perhaps Barson realised he had blown his chance of greatness by leaving the Villa. If he had not been stubborn in 1922 and had channelled his aggressiveness, might Frank Barson have been a Villa great?

BENT, Darren Ashley

Position: Forward
Born: London, Monday 6 February 1984
Career: Youth player, Godmanchester Rovers; Ipswich Town (apprentice, 1998–2001, professional, 2001–05); Charlton Athletic (£3.5 million, 2005–07); Tottenham Hotspur (£16.5

million, 2007–09), Sunderland (£10 million, plus add ons, rising to £16 million over time, 2009–11); ASTON VILLA (£18 million, rising to £24 million with add ons, 18 January 2011)

England (Up to and including 9 February 2011)
Caps: 8, Won: 6, Lost: 2, Drawn: 0, Goals: 2

Darren Bent is a prolific English striker of Jamaican parents who has made his name as a centre-forward with attitude. His potential is massive, and he has represented England at every level from Under-15 through Under-16, Under-17, Under-19, Under-21 and full international level, without fully establishing himself in the England squad. His move to Villa age 26 gives him a real chance to succeed in the Premiership and at international level.

Bent was brought up in Tooting, London, before the family moved to Huntingdon, Cambridgeshire at the age of 10. He joined the Godmanchester youth team, and was signed by Ipswich at the age of 14 on apprentice forms, after considering a possible career in athletics. He signed professional forms with Ipswich on 2 July 2001. The team was struggling and was relegated from the Premiership, but Bent continued to score goals and in 2003–04 scored 16, bettering this in 2004–05 when he scored 19 to be the club's second highest scorer, aged only 20.

He transferred to Charlton in the Premiership on 1 June 2005 in a deal worth an initial £2.5 million and was the highest scoring Englishman in the Premiership in his first season, 2005–06, with 18 goals (22 overall). In 2006–07 he scored 13 goals in the Premier League, but Charlton were relegated. He moved to Tottenham on 29 June 2007 for a club record fee of £16.5 million, inclusive of add ons, payable over three years. He made 36 appearances in 2007–08, scoring eight goals. He then top scored in 2008–09 with 12 Premiership goals (17 in all competitions), and Harry Rednapp was not happy with his contribution especially when he missed an open goal in January 2009. Tension developed in the player-manager relationship.

In July 2009 Sunderland came in for him, and lengthy negotiations led to Bent posting on the internet accusing the Spurs chairman of holding up the move. He went on 5 August for a fee lower than the Spurs record paid for him two years earlier. His first Sunderland season 2009–10 was excellent, with 25 goals in 40 appearances in all competitions. In the first half of the 2010–11 season he was in good form, and it was a major suprise when in the middle of the transfer window he put in a written transfer request on 17 January 2011 and signed for Villa the following day. Sunderland manager Steve Bruce was unhappy, as he did not appear to have been consulted.

England Career

Darren Bent made excellent progress through the lower levels of the England set up, doing particularly well at Under-21 level. He appeared in 14 games, scoring nine goals. However, his progress at full international level has been in fits and starts up to the move to Villa. He was called up by England manager Eriksson to the squad for the friendly against Denmark on 17 August 2005, but was not played. Eriksson played him on 1 March 2006 against Uruguay in a pre-World Cup match. He did not convince the manager to include him in the 2006 World Cup squad. He was just 22.

After Eriksson was replaced by Steve McLaren, the new manager tried him on 16 August 2006 against Greece, but he did not score, and it was over a year before he gained a third cap, on 21 November 2007. The curious pattern of playing him once a season continued in 2008–09 when he played one match on 19 November 2008 against the Germans, again not scoring after being sent on for Jermaine Defoe in the second half.

In the 2009–10 season he did play two games, the first against Brazil on 14 November 2009. He started but was replaced after 55 minutes by Defoe after Brazil had gone 1–0 ahead. He was tried again on 20 May 2010 but failed to score and was replaced by Joe Cole. It is not suprising the managership had reservations, and while he was included in the 30-strong party for the World Cup he was left out of the final selection. At 26 he was behind other strikers in the pecking order.

England's failure in the 2010 World Cup opened a door, especially with the retirement of Emile Heskey as the main centre-forward. He was picked for 7 September 2010 against Switzerland and in his seventh international finally scored. He was left out against Montenegro and France in the next two matches but recalled for the friendly against Denmark on 9 February 2011. He scored his second England goal – an easy tap in from a Theo Walcott cross – but as Bent knows from his Tottenham days, open goals are not unmissable. He played for the whole game and looked impressive in a game where Villa ended with three current players on the pitch.

Bent started for the Wales European Championship on 9 March, scoring England's second goal from an Ashley Young cross. While he was rested for the friendly against Ghana at the end of the month, he clearly is firmly in Fabio Capello's future plans.

Following the Denmark game, his ex-manager Steve Bruce again complained about his transfer, this time over claims that Capello told Bent his chances of selection would be improved if he moved to Villa. Bruce agued with Capello, not Bent, complaining that Capello had not been to the Stadium of Light for 20 months – it was too out of the way. It was a confirmation that Mr Capello does come to Villa Park.

BERESFORD, Joseph

Position: Forward
Born: Chesterfield, 26 February 1906
Died: Birmingham, 26 February 1978
Career: Mansfield Town (May 1926); ASTON VILLA (May 1927); Preston North End (September 1935); Swansea Town (December 1937); Stourbridge (August 1938).
Beresford retired from Stourbridge in 1942. He had also guested for Hartlepool during World War Two.

England

Caps: 1, Won: 0, Lost: 1, Drawn: 0

Another of Villa's 'lost' players, Beresford played for eight years (1927–35) at inside or centre-forward without really making a major impact. He scored 73 goals in 251 first-class matches, which was respectable without being spectacular, and he suffered from being in the same team as Billy Walker and Pongo Waring, both legends. In consequence there was little written about him that has survived. Clearly a reliable and hard-working player, with a reputation as a 'human dynamo', he seems to have been a provider for the better-known players than a scorer in his own right, despite being in two of the highest scoring Villa sides of all time. Capped for England in Prague against the Czechs on 16 May 1934, he had already passed the summit of his career. Perhaps he was prepared to travel at the end of a tiring season when others would not.

His career is very obscure, though he appeared in the two sides which were runners up in the League in 1931 and 1933. Villa's first manager, Jimmy Mullan, transferred him to Preston almost as soon as taking over, ending a career which sadly has left little recorded information behind.

BLACKBURN, George Frederick

Position: Left-half

Born: Willesden Green, London, 18 March 1899

Died: Cheltenham, 2 July 1957

Career: Hamstead Town; Army Football; ASTON VILLA, amateur (December 1920), professional (January 1921); Cardiff City (July 1926); Mansfield Town (June 1931); Cheltenham Town, player-manager (May 1932); Moor Green, coach (August 1932–34); Birmingham, trainer, then coach (1937). Blackburn retired from football in May 1948.

England

Caps: 1, Won: 1, Lost: 0, Drawn: 0

George Blackburn played three full seasons for Villa from 1922–25, taking

over as left-half after Frank Moss Snr moved to the other flank. A sound, unspectacular player, he held down a position through safe and steady play, appearing in the FA Cup Final in 1925 when Villa lost to a Newcastle side who had rested most of their players for the League match earlier in the week. His appearance at Wembley may have given him the publicity to win his only cap in Paris the following month, however. A single cap is not a career, and he peaked with this achievement. A year later he was transferred to Cardiff.

Blackburn played six years in the First Division, 145 times for Villa and 116 with Cardiff. Never lucky with honours, he missed Cardiff's sensational 1927 FA Cup victory over Arsenal. He was, however, a football man through and through and stayed in the game after his career at the top finished and he dropped through the

divisions, returning to Birmingham to coach for over 11 years but at the Blues, not the Villa. His career overall seems to have been one of high competence rather than brilliance, and his career records are limited in the information they contain.

BRAWN, William Frederick

Position: Outside-right
Born: Wellingborough, 1 August 1874
Died: London, 18 August 1932
Career: Wellingborough White Star; Wellingborough Principals; Northampton Town (July 1895); Sheffield United, professional (January 1900); ASTON VILLA (December 1901); Middlesbrough (March 1906); Chelsea (November 1907); Brentford (August 1911).
Brawn retired in May 1919 after guesting for Tottenham Hotspur in World War One. He was later the advisory manager at Griffin Park.

England
Caps: 2, Won: 1, Lost: 0, Drawn: 1

One of the more obscure of the players of the Golden Age before World War One because of the lack of information, William Brawn was a man who was highly respected but who never hit the heights, despite a Cup-winners' medal. A classic late

developer, he played in minor clubs in the south Midlands until he was picked up by Sheffield United in 1900, when he was 26, and he moved to Villa the following year. He played five seasons and was well over 31 when he transferred to Middlesbrough. He won a Cup-winners' medal with Villa in 1905, and presumably Villa thought his best years were past when he was transferred. The eyewitness account in the *Villa News & Record* later that year, when memories of him were fresh, concedes that at his peak he was the best outside-right in the country. It suggests he had more energy than skill, though, which cannot be entirely true. Was this sour grapes for releasing him too soon?

Brawn won two caps at his peak in 1904. He did not score in either of his two games, though England scored five goals, a respectable total. His scoring record for Villa – 20 in 107 appearances – suggests a provider rather than a scorer. The archives divulge little about his playing style, but they do reveal his height, which at 6ft 2in was tall for a winger, and that he could use both feet 'scoring and making goals'.

Villa News & Record 1, 1 September 1906
For a period quite the best outside-right in the country. Possessing a fine turn of speed, is always a dangerous man when once clear. Centres with force and precision from the line, and can shoot with deadly effect when within range. Has scored many fine goals with oblique shots. Brilliant on his day, but somewhat unequal. Forceful, energetic; has more vim than resource.

BROOME, Frank Henry

Position: Forward
Born: Berkhamstead, Herts, 11 June 1915
Died: Bournemouth, 10 September 1994
Career: Berkhamstead Victoria C of E schools; Boxmore United juniors & seniors (September 1929–May 1932); Berkhamstead Town (August 1932); Aston Villa (November 1934); Derby County (1946); Notts County (October 1949); Brentford (July 1953); Crewe (October 1953); Shelbourne (February 1953).

Frank Broome is Villa's 'invisible' international. Despite appearing in one of the most controversial football incidents ever, the 'Hitler Salute' international of 1938, playing at the highest level with some of the greatest names in English soccer history, Broome and his international record is largely unknown today.

He never became a big name, perhaps because when he made his breakthrough in 1938, Villa had only just got promoted from the Second Division and, though highest scorer, he was overshadowed by players like Alex Massie, George Cummings and Eric Houghton. Sadly, when he was in his prime League football was suspended and his war record does not count. Officially he only played 151 games, scoring 91 goals – which is a remarkable goal every 100 minutes.

Frank was a small, speedy winger who could also play inside or centre-forward. He was short – only 5ft 7in – and skinny. In the Villa squad for the 1936–37 season, when he was 21, he weighed only 9st 8lb, the lightest player in a squad of 31 players. (*Villa News & Record*, 29 August 1936 p.3). But like Ashley Young, he was resilient and proved himself a goal machine from the moment he signed in 1934, aged only 19. Peter Morris notes he 'came as an unknown junior from Berkhamstead that autumn [1934] and immediately showed his quality

Broome also guested for Birmingham, Chelmsford City and Wolverhampton Wanderers, during World War Two. He stopped playing in June 1955 on his 40th birthday. He then worked as a coach or manager in England and Australia, then coaching appointments in the Middle East until April 1973. A football man through and through.

England

Caps: 7, Won: 4, Lost: 1, Drawn: 2, Goals: 3

with six goals in a 15-goal drubbing of Moor Green in a Birmingham Combination match'. (p.150)

Broome was the star of the side that won the Second Division Championship in 1938, the top scorer with 26 goals. The programme records that when the final whistle went, the crowd 'called for the players and management. Eventually our captain, James Allen, and Frank Broome...appeared in the directors box, and then the crowd really let itself go'. (*Villa News & Record*, 14 May 1938). By the time that report appeared, he had been called up for England.

The England selectors sent Broome to play a friendly against Germany. The English players went to Berlin seeing this as just a game. They discovered there was no such thing as a friendly match in Nazi Germany. Two months before, Hitler had occupied Austria, Europe was drifting towards war, tension was high. Leading Nazis were at the match and the British ambassador ordered the English players to give the Nazi salute. With 100,000 Nazis in the stadium, the players had no choice. It would be a baptism of fire for Broome.

He rose to the challenge. To make his first England game more difficult, he was ordered to abandon his normal wing role and play as a roving central forward. In the first minute he forced a save from the goalkeeper. At 2–1 to England, Broome fastened onto a long ball out of defence, took it past a German defender 'like a trout slipping past a rock' according to the *Sunday Dispatch* reporter, and scored his first goal for England. It was a step to the eventual 6–3 victory. Astonishingly, he played for Villa the very next day in the same Berlin stadium in another friendly. Aston Villa's players did not give the Nazi salute.

He played six more games for England, including the last three internationals of 1939 alongside men like Tommy Lawton and Stanley Matthews He was clearly an established international with a glittering future ahead of him. But on 3 September 1939 the war began, and football was suspended.

Broome continued to play in the war. Though he added a wartime England appearance to the seven caps he had already won, this was not official and his international career was already over. He won medals in the Wartime League Cup in 1942 and Wartime League North Championship, but he played with scratch teams and he lost his best years.

The Villa encyclopaedia refers to Broome as having an 'intriguing career'. Unfulfilled is a better word for a player who occupied four different forward positions in his eight England games, playing a flexible role for his first game – and who was still representing England at FA level in

1951. It is remarkable he has been almost totally forgotten.

BROWN, Arthur Alfred

Position: Forward
Born: Aston, Birmingham, 15 March 1859
Died: Aston, July 1909
Career: Aston Park School; Florence FC (1874); Aston Unity (1876); ASTON VILLA (August 1878); Michell St Georges (August 1879); Birchfield Trinity; Excelsior FC; ASTON VILLA (February 1880–May 1886). Retired due to ill health but still remained on the staff until 1908.

England

Caps: 3, Won: 1, Lost: 2, Drawn: 0, Goals: 4

Arthur Brown is the key example of the Aston footballer of the early years. It is easy to be romantic about the club in the first dozen years of its existence, before professionalism and the League system, but the club did not really get going till the 1887 Cup victory. At this time Villa was a community club, and both he and his brother were local Aston players who came to the club from what was a very small talent pool. He was small – 5ft 8in – strong and was immensely popular, working as a coach and on the ground staff, something which endeared him to the club's board and supporters.

It is difficult to make any assessment of the early players because of the lack of records. Officially, he only played 22 FA Cup matches. We do not know how many friendlies he played, though he must have played in dozens. Though AA scored 15 goals in FA Cup matches and four in his first international, the 13–0 rout of Ireland in the first, pioneering match against the Irish, his career was not spectacular. He did not score in the two games after the rout of the Irish – defeats by Scotland and Wales – and retired before the 1887 FA Cup win and the transformation of Villa into a fully professional club. All his caps came in early 1882 so his international career only lasted two months. The *Villa Record* praises his impact in these games but notes honours were few in his career. An underachiever or just unlucky?

Villa News & Record 1, 1 September 1906

For his size, probably the most brilliant and successful player produced in the Midlands. In his day he had no local rival, and was scarcely overshadowed by his great captain, Archie Hunter. As a pair, they were simply formidable in many games as centre-forwards. Full of grit, good-tempered, and a magnificent worker, he shone in any company. Made a big mark in international games, and was not exactly overburdened with honours.

BROWN, George

Position: Centre-forward
Born: Mickley, Northumberland, 22 June 1903
Died: Birmingham, 10 June 1948
Career: Mickley Colliery; Huddersfield Town (triallist March 1921, professional April 1921); ASTON VILLA (£5,000, August 1929); Burnley (£1,400, October 1934), Leeds United (£3,100, September 1935); Darlington (£1,000, player-manager, October 1936–October 1938). Retired from football and became pub manager in Birmingham.

England

Caps: 9, Won: 4, Lost: 2, Drawn: 3, Goals: 5

George Brown was a prolific goalscorer, hitting 276 in 444 games

between 1921 and 1938. His form earned him eight caps before moving to Villa in August 1929, and with a superb record for Huddersfield – then managed by a genius, Herbert Chapman – he appeared on the crest of a wave. He had scored 159 goals in 229 games, in a supremely successful team. Villa paid £5,000 for him – big money when their record was £7,500 for Jimmy Gibson in 1927.

Brown should have been at his peak when he signed for Villa aged 26 in 1929, but he seems to have left his best form behind at the Huddersfield. This small club were League Champions in 1924, 1925 and 1926, and runners up in 1927 and 1928. The club dropped to 16th in 1929, as the legendary Chapman had left for Arsenal and with the Villa at third that

season, Brown may well have thought he was making a good career move, but the Villa move was not an ideal one. He scored 89 in only 126 senior games, which is a good ratio, but over five years meant he played an average of 25 games a season – a poor appearance record at a time when clubs played 42 League games a season. He added only one more England cap to the eight he had won at Huddersfield.

He scored a memorable goal in a Cup tie against Arsenal in 1931, and five in an 8–3 beating of Leicester City in January 1932, but Peter Morris suggests he was seen as a substitute for Pongo Waring when the latter was injured, and that they did not work well together – perhaps too similar as centre-forwards. Morris does not say why the combination was not successful.

Eye-witness account:

'He led the forwards with great success when Waring was out through injury for a long spell but when the latter recovered and the Villa tried the two of them together in attack the move was not a success.' (*Aston Villa*, Peter Morris, 1960, p.138)

COLLYMORE, Stanley Victor

Position: Striker
Born: Groundslow Hospital, Swynnerton, Stone, 22 January 1971

Career: Longmoor Boys, Walsall, (YTS June 1989), Wolverhampton Wanderers (non-contract July 1989), Stafford Rangers (July 1990), Crystal Palace (£100,000 December 1990), Southend United, (£100,000 November 1992), Nottingham Forest (£2.25 million July 1993), Liverpool (£8.5 million June 1995), VILLA (£7 million May 1997), Fulham (on loan July 1999), Leicester City (£250,000 rising to £500,000 February 2000), Bradford City (Free transfer October 2000), Real Oviedo Spain (Free transfer January–March 2001, quit claiming might enter politics). Became a sports commentator. From 2008–09 season wrote column in the Villa programme.

England

Caps: 3, Won: 2, Lost: 1, Drawn: 0, Goals: 0

Stan Collymore is one of the most enigmatic players ever to play for Aston Villa. A player with all the best qualities of a modern centre-forward, his arrival was hailed when he was transferred from Liverpool in May 1997. Villa supporters, eager to have a local hero, embraced him wholeheartedly. At one time a huge banner hung from the Holte End, at least 30ft by 20ft with the name Collymore stitched to it in huge white letters on a background of claret-and-blue stripes.

Alas, Collymore was a controversial character. It was rumoured that

managers found him difficult to handle. He was certainly regarded as part of the 'Spice Boys' era at Liverpool when the Liverpool players were prominent parts of the London celebrity scene. Jamie Carragher, in his illuminating autobiography, refers to 'the enigmatic talent of Stan Collymore', one of his milder comments (*Carra*, 2009, p.116). Collymore won two England caps in June 1995, but he did not succeed at Anfield, and Liverpool accepted a loss on their investment in the transfer to Villa.

When Villa spent a record £7 million, he was seen as the missing piece of the jigsaw to lift them to the top. Brian Little's team had won the League Cup in 1996 and in 1997 had finished fifth. Collymore's signing was heralded as the spark for a challenge for the title. Instead, Villa lost the first four matches and were struggling in 15th in February 1998 when Brian Little shocked the club by resigning.

Rumours of rifts in the dressing room surfaced in the media, but have been denied by Brian Little, who stated 'If Stan had a cold, the press would say he's off with something else. Stan's a lovely man, a lovely lad. He's just made one or two bad decisions'. (Woodall, p.197) Indeed, Sasa Curcic's problems not Collymore's were seen as being to blame for Brian Little's decision to quit.

John Gregory, the new manager, was initially sympathetic to a player who had won a third cap on 10 September 1997. Two weeks before Christmas 1998 Collymore hit the high spots when coming off the bench to spark an astonishing recovery against Arsenal who having led 2–0 at half time were beaten 3–2. Sadly, there were few such high points. Gregory's patience was tried after a media storm over an incident involving Collymore's then girlfriend, Ulrika Johnson, and relations deteriorated. In the New Year of 1998 Collymore claimed to be suffering from depression. (Woodall, p.207) Gregory had little sympathy with depression and relations deteriorated.

After a loan spell with Fulham in 1999 there was a very public row, and from the middle of October 1999 for the next four months Collymore played no football at all. In February of the 1999–2000 season, which started badly but ended up with Villa at Wembley for the Cup, Collymore was transferred to Martin O'Neill's Leicester for a nominal fee. According to the *Complete Record*, he played for Villa 1997–99 but he was on the books until February 2000. The missing four months are a mystery. It is clear Collymore was an item at Villa for more than two years, and his Villa record of 61 games – 12 as substitute – and 15 goals was a poor return. He did not score for England, and overall he failed to fulfil his potential.

COWANS, Gordon Sidney

Position: Left-midfield
Born: Cornforth, County Durham, 27 October 1958
Career: ASTON VILLA, apprentice (July 1974), professional (August 1976); Bari, £450,000 (1985); ASTON VILLA, £250,000 (July 1988); Blackburn Rovers, £200,000 (November 1991); ASTON VILLA, free transfer (July 1993); Derby County, £80,000 (February 1994);

Wolverhampton Wanderers, £20,000 (December 1994); Sheffield United, free transfer (December 1995); Bradford City, free transfer (July 1996); Stockport County, free transfer (March 1997); Burnley, reserve team player-coach, free transfer (August 1997–May 1998); ASTON VILLA, assistant manager-coach (August 1998). **See Pantheon section for full details.**

CRABTREE, James

Position: Left-half (started career at left-back)
Born: Burnley, 23 December 1871
Died: Birmingham, 18 June 1908
Career: Burnley Royal Swifts (1885); Burnley (August 1889); Rossendale (August 1890); Heywood Central (July 1891); Burnley (Professional) August 1892; ASTON VILLA (£250 August 1895); Plymouth Argyle (January–April 1904). Crabtree retired as a player May 1904, coached several non-League clubs for two years before becoming a pub landlord in 1906, two years before his untimely death aged only 36.

England

Caps: 14, Won: 9, Lost: 2, Drawn: 3, Goals: 0

Crabtree was signed from Burnley in the close season of 1895 for a then club record fee of £250 and a reputation of being a great left-back and already the possessor of three caps for England. However, Spencer and Welford were in possession of the full-back positions and Crabtree was persuaded to move to centre-half. He converted to this position and became a great half-back as a result.

Crabtree was an essential player in the most successful Villa team of all time, appearing in 202 games for the all-conquering side of the late 1890s in which he won Championship medals in 1896, 1897, 1899 and 1900, and helped to win the Cup and the double in 1897. Some books say he was captain of Burnley, Villa and England, but the records show he was never captain of England in the 14 games he played for the national side. There is also an unexplained gap of three years, April 1896 to February 1899, when he did not win any caps. Given that this covered Villa's famous double year (1896–97) this is very odd.

Crabtree is something of an enigma, although he was seen as a massively talented player. When he retired, Gibson and Pickford asked him to write an essay on 'great forward lines I have known' and in *The Book of Football*, published in the same year of 1906, he contributed a chapter on the skill of half-back play. In March 1896 he was the only Villa player from the double side to be selected for the famous Players team against the Corinthians in the annual Gentlemen versus Players game,

playing alongside such great professionals as Bassett, Bloomer and Goodall, and suprisingly selected at right-back. Illness and withdrawals meant that he actually played at centre-half, and the biography of G.O. Smith, the famous captain from Oxford University, notes casually that Crabtree 'could play in any position'.

Despite his enormous ability, there was an unexplained fragility to Crabtree's mental and physical state. He is said to have had fits, some serious, and was very sensitive to criticism, storming off in a temper in an argument. He is also rumoured to have had a drink problem and died at the very early age of 36. Perhaps becoming a pub landlord in Lozells was not the best retirement plan.

Villa News & Record 1, 1 September 1906
'One of England's greatest players. Shone in any position. Great as a half-back, but greater, possibly, as a back, kicking cleanly and with rare precision…A keen, skilful tackler, clever at close quarters, and equally reliable in the open: cool, resourceful and brainy. Excelled in the finer points of the game, and one of the most versatile players England has ever boasted.'

DALEY, Anthony Mark

Position: Left or right wing
Born: Birmingham, 18 October 1967

Career: Aston Manor School; Holte Comprehensive School; Birmingham Boys; ASTON VILLA, YTS (June 1983), professional (May 1985); Wolverhampton Wanderers, £1.25 million (June 1994); Watford (July 1998); FC Madeira, Portugal; Hapoel Haifa FC, Cyprus; Walsall (June 1999); Nailsworth FC; Forest Green Rovers (October 1999).

England
Caps: 7, Won: 2, Lost: 1, Drawn: 4

An Aston lad – just like the 'Good Old Days' of Ramsey and Rinder – who signed as a YTS apprentice from school at the age of 16, Tony Daley made his breakthrough aged 17 in

April 1985 in a 5–2 home win over QPR. Daley was a massively talented player and signed a three-year contract that May. He started to reach his full potential when Graham Taylor took over as manager after Billy McNeill in the spring of 1986, when Villa finished bottom of the old First Division and were in free fall.

Taylor had a brilliant ability to coach individual players to improve their skills – Gordon Cowans regarded him as 'probably the most thorough manger I've played under' (McColl p.126) – and Tony Daley was one who benefited immensely from the new manager's coaching. Paradoxically, his very speed was a problem and Derek Mountfield commented when Villa got back into the upper tier, 'Tony has to be one of the fastest wingers in the First Division. The manager has been coaching him closely, trying to get him to slow down a bit just before he crosses the ball' (McColl p.128). Daley listened to the manager, played a slower game, and became an international player as a result. After England's elimination from the 1990 World Cup, Bobby Robson resigned and Graham Taylor was promoted to be England manager. It was natural he would consider Tony Daley as part of his rebuilding for the European Championship campaign.

The new Villa manager, Ron Atkinson, made Tony Daley a key player, and Daley was a star of Atkinson's first season, 1991–92. This encouraged Taylor to call Daley into the England squad, winning his first cap as a substitute after 70 minutes of the European qualifier against Poland on 13 November 1991. Daley was left on the sidelines for the next two England games, but he was in Taylor's thoughts and gained a second cap against the CIS in Moscow on 29 April 1992. He won two more caps against Hungary and Brazil in friendlies, but he had become an impact player to be used against tiring defences.

Daley was in the Euro squad but only used as a substitute in the first game, a 0–0 draw against Denmark. He couldn't break down the Danish defence in the 25 minutes he was on the pitch, and he was dropped for the second game. This was also a 0–0 draw meaning the third game, against Sweden, had to be won. Platt scored in the third minute, but England were dire and went down 2–1 and out of the competition. Daley had been included in the team but had missed chances, though he could not be blamed: more experienced players failed dismally. This was the match which led to the disgraceful tabloid headline 'Turnips 1, Swedes 2'. Tony Daley never played for England again.

The next season, 1992–93, was disrupted by a knee injury, but he was back for a fine season in 1993–94. He was unsettled and asked for a move in the autumn of 1993, but nothing happened. He played a major part in the 1994 League Cup victory, scoring the decisive penalty in the semi-final, and then undertook a crucial role in a 4–5–1 midfield formation against Manchester United, which successfully counterattacked. Daley left for Wolves the summer of 1994 with a League Cup-winners' medal and an excellent career in the Villa first team.

DEVEY, John Henry George

Position: Forward
Born: Newtown, Birmingham, 26 December 1866
Died: Birmingham, 13 October 1940
Career: Various youth sides; Aston Unity; Aston Manor; West Bromwich Albion (briefly 1889); Mitchell's St George (1890); ASTON VILLA (professional March 1891). Retired in April 1901, coach 1901–03, club director June 1904–September 1934.

He also played county cricket for Warwickshire 1888–97, scoring over 6,500 first-class runs. Later ran a sports outfitters shop in Lozells.
A remarkably skilful player and goalscorer who scored with head and both feet, John Devey often scored from long distance when he saw the goalkeeper was off his line. He was a key player of the great Villa team of the 1890s who won the Championship five times and the FA Cup twice, including the double of 1897. He also collected a Cup runners'-up medal in 1892. He reached his peak in the double side of 1897, appearing in 29 of the 30 League games and all seven games in the FA Cup. He scored 186 goals in 308 senior appearances, all for Villa.

As club captain in the golden age of the 1890s, his contribution was more than just as an individual player. At outside-right he had Charlie Athersmith as his partner, who had signed from Unity Gas Depot a month before Devey arrived. They made a formidable pairing on the right wing, and it was Devey who 'made' Athersmith the player he became, much as Billy Walker later 'made' first Arthur Dorrell and then Eric Houghton into England players.

Given his skill, it is disappointing that he was only capped twice for England. The international IFRR study of the England players before World War Two noted he was the 'outstanding regisseur (inspiration) of the world famous "Villains" but he was only selected twice for the national team', which the writer obviously saw as being odd. Those who saw him ranked him highly and unlucky in his caps total. He was given a separate chapter in *The Book of Football* (pp.179–183), the two authors noting it was his bad luck to coincide with John Goodall and Steve Bloomer, two of the greatest inside-forwards of the time. He wrote an article on The Art of Captaincy in *The Book of Football* (1906).

He was a great captain, sportsman and player with a wide range of interests – he actually came to Villa to play baseball, then a popular sport. He never played against Scotland, his great ambition, gaining both caps against Ireland. In March 1892 he played in a 2–0 victory in Belfast, then two years later returned for a 2–2 draw. He scored one goal for England.

Villa News & Record 1, 1 September 1906
'For one so skilful, thorough and effective, his merits when in his prime were inexplicably overlooked by the [England] Selection Committee. Could play in most positions in the forward line, and was for many years one of the very best pivots in England. A close dribbler, with good pace, he was alive to every movement on the field. Knew the game really well, never lacked initiation, but a strong believer in combination.'

DORRELL, Arthur Reginald

Position: Outside-left wing
Born: Small Heath, Birmingham, 30 March 1896
Died: Alum Rock, Birmingham, 14 September 1942
Career: Belper Road School; Leicester; Carey Hall FC, Leicester; RASC, Army service from 1916; ASTON VILLA (May 1919); Port Vale (June 1931).
Dorrell retired in August 1932 to become a pub landlord in Alum Rock.

England

Caps: 4, Won: 3, Lost: 0, Drawn: 1, Goals: 1

Arthur Dorrell was a very popular player in his 12 years at Villa Park. He was regarded as family – his father had also played for the Villa. He joined Villa after war service, in which he had won the Army Sprinting Championships in France, and was partner for Billy Walker on the left once Walker had moved from centre-forward to inside-left. Though celebrated for his speed, he was a

skilful player who provided a headache for opposition defenders. As a conventional winger he was an effective foil to Walker for a remarkable eight seasons. Overall Dorrell competed in 12 seasons, playing 390 first-class games and scoring 65 goals as an old style run-and-cross winger. He played in two Cup Finals, winning in 1920 and losing in 1924.

Apart from his four full caps, he represented the Football League in 1923. A highly respected squad player, Dorrell never achieved the heights as a player but was seen as a reliable and effective player whose name was always on the team sheet at Villa Park. Perhaps he was taken for granted as a virtual ever present who did not need much commentary. He was tried by the international selectors in his prime in his late twenties to partner Walker but he did not have Walker's presence, though he could be relied upon to give of his best whenever called to do so. Villa fans saw him as a player who always worked a full shift – his record shows he missed only five matches in four successive seasons. He almost joined the select band who have played 400 games for the Villa.

DOWNING, Stewart

Position: Left attacking midfield
Born: Middlesbrough 22 July 1984
Career: Middlesbrough (1 August 2001–16 July 2009); Sunderland (loan 29 October 2003–11 December 2003); ASTON VILLA (16 July 2009–present)

England: (Up to and including 9 February 2011)
Caps: 24, Won: 15, Lost: 4, Drawn: 5, Goals: 0

Stewart Downing's career began with great promise at Middlesbrough where he won 23 caps, then hit a downward slide which led him to move to Villa, where he has begun to rebuild his reputation and regained a place in the England squad in late 2010, winning his first cap as a Villa player against Denmark on 9 February 2011.

Downing grew up on Middlesbrough's Pallister estate and supported the club as a schoolboy. He rose through the Middlesbrough Academy and made his Premier League debut on 24 April 2002, aged 18. He was sent out on loan to Sunderland in late 2003 to gain experience. The 2004–05 season saw him break through into the Middlesbrough first team, making 49 appearances with six goals. His form caught Sven-Goran Eriksson's eye, and the then England manager called him up and he gained his first cap on 9 February 2005 – at Villa Park in a friendly against Holland, having already gained seven Under-21 caps after being called up for the 2003 UEFA Under-19 Championship.

Alas, he was injured in May 2005 while training for England on their tour of the US. He was sidelined for five months, but at the end of the 2005–06 season was called up for an England B game, and impressed sufficiently to gain a cap in a friendlly against Jamaica and then a call up for the 2006 World Cup, where he won three caps.

With Eriksson replaced after the World Cup by Steve McLaren, it was not suprising that Downing continued to be called up by the ex-Middlesbrough manager. There was criticism that his form did not justify his caps, but by the time Capello took over he had won over the critics.

Capello was impressed by Downing and kept selecting him. But by the time he won his 23rd cap, against Slovakia on 28 March 2009, Downing was caught up in the turmoil at his home club.

Steve McLaren had been replaced as Middlesbrough manager by Gareth Southgate, and the ex-Boro and Villa star could not provide success at the Riverside. An awful winless run started in November 2008 and Boro fell into the relegation zone. On 5 January 2009 Downing handed in a written transfer request. This was rejected, and Downing played in every game bar the last match, a 2–1 defeat at West Ham which relegated them. He could not be blamed for the relgation. He had contributed 362 crosses, not far behind Ashley Young's record that Premier season of 377. And he did not play in the final crucial game because he had been injured playing against Villa – by Stilian Petrov – and needed an operation, which put him out for four months.

During this period, Martin O'Neill signed him for a club-record £12 million in July 2009. Despite criticism over a signing of an injured player, he came back in November 2009 and immediately began to win over the fans. His second season, 2010–11, started well and he was called up by Capello for the Euro 2010 qualifier against Montenegro on 12 October

2010 but did not start. He continued to play well for Villa and was called into the squad for a friendly against Denmark. He was sent on as a substitute on 9 February 2011, exactly six years to the day since he had won his first cap. He ended the game as Villa's 71st capped player, alongside Ashley Young and Darren Bent. When he had signed for Villa, he is said to have asked if he was being signed to replace Young. He was not. His first cap as a Villa player, on 9 February 2011 against Denmark, saw him replace Theo Walcott on 68 minutes alongside Young and Bent. The international appearance confirmed that the two players do not cancel each other out, for Villa or for England.

Stewart Downing is the latest player to be capped for England while a Villa player, number 71 in the all-time list. He has yet to receive a yellow or red card for England and has a good attitude in line with the behaviour expected of a Villa player. When at Middlesbrough he was involved in several local charitable projects, including the No Messin' campaign warning children against playing on railway lines. Downing held a charity dinner with boxer Ricky Hatton to raise funds for the Newcastle hospital which had cared for his sister Vicky during her fatal illness with cancer, aged four. He has also been a club DJ in his spare time.

DUBLIN, Dion

Position: Striker
Born: Leicester, 22 April 1969
Career: Oakham United; Norwich City, professional (March 1988); Cambridge United, free transfer (August 1988); Manchester United, £1 million (August 1992); Coventry City, £2 million (September 1994); ASTON VILLA, £5.75 million (November 1998); Millwall, on loan (March–May 2008); Leicester City (May 2004).

Dublin ended his career back at Norwich.

England
Caps: 4, Won: 2, Lost: 1, Drawn:

Dion Dublin won one cap while playing with the Villa, on 18 November 1998, a match that also saw Paul Merson finish his England career and Lee Hendrie gain his one England cap. With three Villa players in an England side, it looked as though Villa were breaking through as an international force. Alas, it was not to be.

Dublin was a late developer as a footballer. He started at Norwich City but, like David Platt, did not achieve his potential and was transferred on a free to Cambridge United when he was 19. Again like Platt, dropping down the divisions allowed him to develop, and in three seasons he scored 73 goals in 201 appearances, a very respectable total, and gained a Third Division Championship (currently League One) in 1991. Manchester United were sufficiently impressed to sign him as a 23-year-old. Unfortunately, he broke his leg and was out for five months. When he came back he found Eric Cantona blocking his progress. He transferred to Coventry, where he scored 72 goals in 171 appearances, earned three caps in the 1998 season and made the move to Villa.

At Villa he started brilliantly, winning the last of his England caps, and briefly formed a promising partnership with Stan Collymore. He was scoring regularly until 18 December 1999, when he was taken off after a clash of heads. The Villa staff took the routine precaution of putting him in a neck brace and saved his life. The hospital found that he had broken his neck. Amazingly, Dublin returned before the end of the season fully recovered, and he appeared in the 2000 Cup Final.

Brave and hard working though he was, he did not quite come up to expectations, however, in part because the 5–3–2 formation favoured by manager John Gregory meant the strikers didn't get enough assists and there were too many balls for the forwards to chase without support. Dublin became an isolated figure long before his loan to Millwall effectively ended his career, with Juan Pablo Angel preferred as the main strike-forward. Always a hard-working player, very popular with the fans, Dublin never quite fulfilled the promise of his major transfers.

DUCAT, Andrew

Position: Right-half
Born: Brixton, Surrey, 16 February 1886
Died: Lords Cricket Ground, Marylebone, London, 23 July 1942
Career: Westcliff Athletic; Southend Athletic; Woolwich Arsenal, amateur (January 1905), professional (February 1905); ASTON VILLA, £1,000 (June 1912); Fulham (May 1921–May 1924), manager (May 1924–26); Corinthian Casuals, amateur.

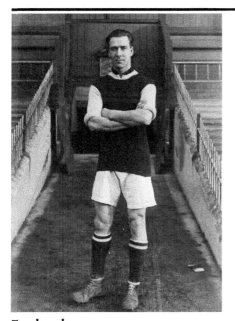

England

Caps: 6, Won: 3, Lost: 2, Drawn: 1, Goals: 1

Andy Ducat was one of the last of the old-style Victorian footballers for whom sport was a calling as much as a job. Though he became professional, he played in the Corinthian spirit of the game as a way of life, and it was fitting that after his professional career he was reinstated as the amateur he had been at the start of his career to play for the Casuals. His sporting character and reputation as never having been sent off or booked earned him a post as a games master at Eton, though this was as cricket coach – Ducat was one of the rare breed who played soccer in the winter and county cricket in the summer. He was also part of an even

smaller group of players capped for England at both sports. Nonetheless, while on Villa's payroll, he always worked a full shift and never shirked his responsibilities to the team.

Ducat was one of three players who spanned World War One for both Villa and England, the others being Sam Hardy and Charlie Wallace. Ducat was playing for Woolwich Arsenal when he won his first three caps in 1910 at the age of 24. Villa noted him and signed him in June 1912 for a then club record fee of £1,000. His start at Villa was hampered by a broken leg, though, sustained in only his fourth Villa game, which kept him out for the best part of two years and meant he missed the 1913 Cup Final and was prevented from winning caps for England in this period. He did not return until 5 September 1914, in a season which was the last before the war brought sport to an end. Remarkably, he returned to top flight football for the Villa in 1919–20, when soccer resumed after the war, though he was 33 in 1919. Despite his age he captained Villa to victory in the 1920 Cup Final.

Although he only played a limited number of games before being transferred to Fulham in 1921, his reputation was outstanding and it was fitting he was captain for the 1920 Cup Final victory. His recall by England in 1920 to play in March, April and

October 1920, the last two on the winning side, may have been due to a lack of experienced players after the war, but he rose to the challenge and did not let England down.

Andy Ducat was a sportsman through and through, with an excellent record in county cricket. He played 25 years for Surrey (1906–31), mainly as a batsman, averaging 38.63 in 428 first-class matches. He played in one test, and fittingly, if tragically, died from a heart attack while batting at Lords in 1942, aged 56.

EHIOGU, Ugochuku 'Ugo'

Position: Centre-half (defender)
Born: Hackney Marshes, London, 3 November 1972
Career: West Bromwich Albion, YTS (1988), professional (July 1989); ASTON VILLA, (£40,000, July 1991); Middlesbrough, (£8 million, October 2000).

England

Caps: 4, Won: 2, Lost: 2, Drawn: 0, Goals: 1

Ugo Ehiogu was a commanding central defender who worked particularly well in partnership with Gareth Southgate. He was signed by West Bromwich Albion after he left school as a YTS apprentice, but to Villa's great benefit they could not or would not hold on to him and sold him for a derisory fee. As with David Platt's transfer to Crewe, however, someone must have suspected a high degree of potential because they inserted a 25 per cent sell-on clause into the contract, earning the Baggies £2 million later in his career.

Ugo had a successful career at Villa, earning 15 caps at Under-21 level and appearing at B team level. He also gained the first of his caps while at Villa. He gained a League Cup-winners' medal in the 1996 Final against Leeds when it was called the Coca-Cola Cup, helping a solid Villa defence keep a clean sheet in a 3–0 victory. While other dressing room disputes led to manager Brian Little's resignation in 1998, Ehiogu and Southgate formed a rock at the heart of the defence

Sadly, the partners found working with new manager John Gregory difficult, and in autumn 2000 a disagreement with Gregory over being left out of the team led to Ugo being transferred to Middlesbrough for a massive £8 million. At the time this made him the second most expensive defender in British football, behind Manchester United's Jaap Stam. The following summer Gareth Southgate followed him to recreate their partnership at the Riverside.

Ugo won one cap while with Villa, coming on as a sub for the friendly against Bulgaria on 27 March 1996, substituting for captain Tony Adams in the 77th minute. Thirteen minutes was not enough to make an impact, but the move to Middlesbrough resurrected his England career, and he was picked for two friendlies in 2001 and one in 2002. He did not establish himself, however, and he joined the ranks of those players who were very good club players but not fully convincing on the international stage. Ugo was unfortunate that he had to compete with players of the quality of Tony Adams and Sol Campbell for a place in the England squad.

GARDNER, Thomas

Position: Wing-half
Born: Huyton, 28 May 1909
Died: May 1970
Career: Orrell 1926; Liverpool (amateur July 1928, professional April

1929); Grimsby Town (May 1931); Hull City (May 1932); ASTON VILLA (£4,500, February 1934); Burnley (April 1938), guested for Blackpool in World War Two, Wrexham (December 1945), Wellington Town (August 1947), Oswestry Town (player-manager 1950), reverting to player-coach January 1952), Chester (assistant trainer July 1954–May 1967). Gardner was a steward at Chester FC for 12 months before becoming a hotelier in Wrexham. He had guested for Blackpool in World War Two.

England
Caps: 2, Won: 1, Lost: 1, Drawn: 0, Goals: 0

Gardner was a player who never hit the high spots in his career, moving around without every making a significant mark. He was one of the players bought just before Jimmy McMullan was appointed Villa's first manager, and sold by Jimmy Hogan four years later. He arrived having gained a Third Division North Championship medal with Hull in May 1933, spending little more than half a season in Division Two with Hull. Villa had begun to slide and he thus joined a team only capable of mid table mediocrity in the First Division, its position at the end of the 1933–34 season.

The Villa maintained this in 1934–35 under McMullan, but was then relegated at the end of the 1935–36 season. McMullan was sacked and Hogan appointed manager in November 1936, getting the club back to the First Division as champions of Division Two in May 1938. He sold Gardner to Burnley, six places below them in Division Two that season, as he had no belief Gardner would contribute to a promotion push.

Gardner only made 79 appearances for Villa in four seasons, partly due to constant injuries which meant he could not develop a consistent pattern of play. He was renowned for a long throw and won a *Daily Mail* competition in 1932 – throwing a ball 40m with wind assistance. He is remembered for little more, though he clearly had a reasonable level of skill.

He was capped in May 1934 for an away match against Czechoslovakia in Prague, just after arriving at Villa, and was recalled almost exactly a year later against the Dutch in Amsterdam. It is difficult to know why he only played two matches, and equally difficult not to feel that overseas matches at the end of the season are not attractive to top players after a long season. But this is speculation. All that can really be said is that Gardner was a committed player, but not really out of the top drawer.

GARRATTY, William

Position: Centre-forward
Born: Saltley, Birmingham, 6 October 1878
Died: Birmingham, 6 May 1931
Career: Church Road and St Saviour's Schools, Birmingham; Highfield Villa; Lozells FC; Aston Shakespeare; ASTON VILLA, professional (August 1897); Leicester Fosse (September 1908); West Bromwich Albion (£270, October 1908); Lincoln City (£100, November 1910).

Garratty retired in May 1911 and was thereafter a beer delivery driver for Ansells Brewery until his death.

England

Caps: 1, Won: 1, Lost: 0, Drawn: 0

In the nine years Garratty played for the Villa he proved a highly effective forward, proving one of the links

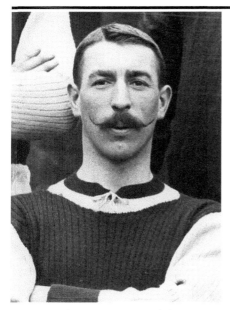

catching players, inside and outside the club, Garratty has never been remembered as a name player. The *Villa News & Record*, in its review of international players in its first edition in 1906, did not have pen portrait of him, though he had been capped for England against Wales on 2 March 1903. He was taken for granted, though without players like him Villa would not have been the successful club it was.

GEORGE, William (Billy)

Position: Goalkeeper
Born: Shrewsbury, 29 June 1874
Died: Birmingham, 4 December 1931
Career: Woolwich Ramblers (1894); army service with Royal Artillery

between the great team of the 1890s and the team which won the FA Cup in 1905. He joined immediately after the Double season of 1897 and was part of the brilliant attack which included Athersmith, Devey, Wheldon and Steve Smith – all of whom gained caps – and he played in the 1899 and 1900 Championship sides. He ended the latter season as the top scorer in the country with 27 goals from only 33 matches, an excellent haul. He then played in the same team as Joe Bache, and later played with the young Harry Hampton. His 259 appearances netted 112 goals, a very good record which deserved more credit.

Garratty was one of those essential squad players on which the more brilliant players depend. Perhaps because he was overshadowed by other more eye-

(February 1895); Trowbridge Town (during army days, 1895–97); ASTON VILLA (£50, professional October 1897); Birmingham, player-trainer (July 1911).

George retired as a player in 1913. He also played cricket for Warwickshire (1901, 1902 and 1907), Wiltshire and Shropshire.

England

Caps: 3, Won: 1, Lost: 0, Drawn: 2

Billy George was signed in 1897 out of the army, causing a minor scandal, after impressive performances on leave for Trowbridge Town. Ramsey and Rinder, involved in the controversial signing and suspended for a month for malpractice, were justified because he became a highly rated goalkeeper who played for 12 years, making 396 appearances. His first appearance against West Brom in 9 October 1897 became legendary, and he was then first choice until 1909. He helped the club win the 1899 and 1900 Championships and the 1905 FA Cup.

George was a big man – one of the few players of the time over 6ft and with an ample waistline. It is recorded that he was 21st 7lb, though this is hard to believe and a weight of 14st is more credible. Whatever the scales said, he was light on his feet. At the height of his career Charlie Johnstone wrote: 'It is wonderful what a sense of security one feels with George in goal. There may be more spectacular custodians but all through his long career I know of no one who has been so consistently safe and reliable.' (*Sporting Mail,* 16 November 1907)

He officially played only three games for England, the three home internationals of 1902, and although in unbeaten sides, he never played again. He also played in the Scottish game at Ibrox, abandoned after the disaster which claimed 26 lives. After 1902, England experimented with a number of goalies until 1907, when Sam Hardy became their number one – and eventually Villa's choice. Hardy was so good he has overshadowed Billy George. George's record shows he deserves to come out of Hardy's shadow and be recognised as the greatest goalkeeper Villa had in the first three and a half decades of its history. The *Villa News* entry in 1906 summed up how many felt, and only Hardy's arrival made George a forgotten man.

Villa News & Record 1, 1 September 1906

One of the greatest – if not the greatest – goalkeepers in the history of the club. For many seasons was at the top of his form, after a superb opening display against West Bromwich Albion. Quick on his feet, splendid reach, full of resource, punches the ball with great power, fields well, and a grand kick. A rare good man on a side, and an ornament to the game.

GIDMAN, John

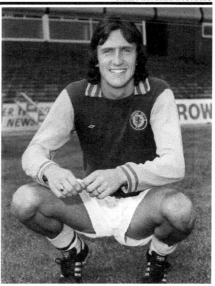

Position: Right-back

Born: Liverpool, 10 January 1954

Career: Garston schoolboy football; Liverpool (apprentice June 1969); ASTON VILLA (professional, August 1971); Everton (£650,000, October 1979); Manchester United (£450,000, August 1981); Manchester City (free transfer, October 1986); Stoke City (August 1988); Darlington (player-assistant manager February–May 1989); Kings Lynn, manager then retired from football.

England

Caps: 1, Won: 1, Lost: 0, Drawn: 0, Goals: 0

When Tommy Docherty left Villa in January 1970, he predicted that while the club was in relegation trouble the youth policy he had set in place would bear fruit in two or three years time. He was right. In 1972 the Villa Youth team won the FA Youth Cup for the first time, producing two outstanding prospects in John Gidman and Brian Little. Gidman was Liverpudlian by birth, but he had not made the grade at Anfield. Villa scout Neville Briggs persuaded him to move to Villa for the 1971–72 season, even though Villa were in the Third Division.

Gidman knocked on the door of the first team as Villa rose through two promotions, though progress was hampered by a firework accident in 1974 which prevented him from playing in the League Cup Final of 1975. He had however won the Terrace Trophy award voted for by fans for the 1973–74 season, proving his popularity with the supporters. Promotion to the old Division One showed he could compete as a pacy wing back – an attacking defender of a kind just making an impact in the modern game. 1976–77 was a splendid season showing him able to get up the field to cross the ball for Little and his other attackers, and then get back to do his defensive duties with speed and efficiency. He helped Ron Saunder's first great side to win the 1977 League Cup. Alas, he fell out with manager Ron Saunders, and after completing 243 senior appearances he was transferred to Everton. He never really succeeded after leaving the Villa, though his 95 games with Manchester

United won him an FA Cup-winners' medal. He later played with his former teammate Brian Little at Darlington.

He represented England at Youth, Under-23, B and full international level, but only won one cap at the highest level. His one cap, against Luxemburg in a World Cup qualifier on 30 March 1977, allowed him to contribute to a 5–0 victory. However, competition for the right back berth was intense, and Luxembourg were not a serious test. Phil Neal of Liverpool was the main contender for the right back berth, and with Liverpool regulars in Europe Neal was more experienced at the highest level. Gidman never won another cap. The anonymous contributor to football-england.com says he was 'a man who, though a defender, always played the game with a great sense of adventure, skill and fun'. Absolutely right.

HALL, Albert Edward

Position: Outside-left
Born: Wordsley, Stourbridge, February 1882
Died: Stourbridge, 17 October 1957
Career: Amblecote Council School; Stourbridge (August 1900); ASTON VILLA (July 1903); Millwall (December 1913–August 1916).

England

Caps: 1, Won: 0, Lost: 1, Drawn: 0

A good club player, there is relatively little information on Albert Hall although he played in very successful teams. He was 21 when he signed for Villa and 31 when he left for Millwall, spending his prime years at the club. He won an FA Cup-winners' medal in 1905 and a League Championship medal in 1910, and he made 215 senior appearances for Villa in his 10 years at the club. He netted 62 goals, being noted more as a maker of goals than a scorer. He was initially an inside-right but made his mark at outside-left partnering Joe Bache. This was a great success for a good five years between 1905–10.

Though Hall could play in any forward position, there is little information on his style of play. He was one of those players who made a solid contribution, allowing the star players to perform. He is described as being 'lightning quick over 20–30 yards' and 'a real box of tricks', which says very little.

Hall was tried for England alongside Bache, who was winning his sixth cap, in the February 1910 match against Ireland, but the experiment was not deemed a success despite the partnership being at its height for Villa, who were on course to win the Championship. There is little information on why Hall was not seen as a successful international player, though he was criticised for overusing the wing trick of waiting for a full-back to challenge before dragging the ball back to beat him. If the back tackled quickly to prevent the drag back, he could get hurt.

Hall did not make enough of a mark to leave behind the information needed for a proper assessment – even the pen portraits in the 1906 *Villa News* do not mention him.

HAMPTON, Harry (Joseph)

Position: centre-forward
Born: Wellington, Shropshire, 24 April 1885,
Died: Wrexham 15 March 1963
Career: Wellington Town, Aston Villa (April 1904), Birmingham (February 1920), Newport County (September 1922-May 1923), retired. Returned for Wellington Town (January 1924), Preston North End (coach, June 1925–January 1926), Birmingham (works football October 1934–April 1936), guested for Derby, Fulham and Notts Forest during World War One.

England
Caps: 4, Won: 2, Lost: 2, Drawn: 0, Goals: 2

'Appy 'Arry 'Ampton, as he was affectionately known, was possibly Villa's greatest goalscorer. His record was superb – 242 goals in 372 appearances in nearly 16 years, but with the years 1915 to 1919 taken out by World War One, the lost years posing the question how many more goals he might have scored for the Villa. Billy Walker scored two more, but in 531 games. Whatever the differences between the game then and now – and it is faster with more challenges from international and Cup games today – these are exceptional achievements. Harry's goals-to-appearances ratio of one goal every 1.54 games or an average of one goal every 64 minutes of play is unlikely to be matched ever.

Hampton was seen as a goalscoring prodigy from the start. He scored both goals in the 2–0 Cup Final victory over Newcastle in 1905 when he was only just 20. He was given a three-page section in the four-volume account of the early years of

football published in 1905. Hampton was the best exponent of the sledgehammer type of centre-forward of the first decades of the League. Hampton played in an era when charging the goalkeeper was seen as fair, and he always tried to barge the goalie into the back of the net if he had the ball. Legend has it he even barged the famous 'Fatty' Foulke of Sheffield United into the back of the net for a goal, and Foulke was said to weigh 22st.

His success in this aggressive style of play is undoubted. He gained Cup-winners' medals in 1905 and 1913, a Championship medal in 1910, and featured in the 1920 Final on the losing side. His return to play after World War One is remarkable given that he had been gassed in the trenches. Despite his choirboy appearance – in the surviving photographs he has the innocent pose of a naughty boy who has just scoffed all the pies – he was clearly as tough as old boots.

Nevertheless, he did not appeal to the selectors. It was not until after Villa's Championship season in 1910 that he was finally given an England trial, in 1911, and did not finally win a cap until after another trial in 1913. He played in two games in 1913, the matches against Scotland and Wales, and another two in 1914. But he was nearly 29, and not an established international. He lost his chance when war stopped international football. When he came back to the Villa in 1919, his best years were behind him. He made his 373rd appearance (Betts p.8) on 3 January 1920. He resented being transferred to Birmingham City, but at 34 his career was declining. A legend for Aston Villa, the leap to international status was never quite achieved.

Villa News & Record, 23 April 1913
'No centre-forward of recent years has maintained for so long such splendid form and yet never departed from the injury-inviting style of play that is essential to success in this position. Hampton has the dash of youth combined with the judgement of experience…When opposed to Hampton, the back who hesitates is lost, and in most cases the goalkeeper is in the same position. He is a man with speed and a fine knowledge of how to use it.'

HARDY, Samuel

Position: Goalkeeper
Born: Newbould Verdun, Derbyshire, 25 August 1883
Died: Chesterfield, 24 November 1966
Career: Newbould White Star (July 1901); Chesterfield (professional, April 1903); Liverpool (£500, October 1905); ASTON VILLA (May 1912); Nottingham Forest (August 1921–May 1925)

England

Caps: 21, Won: 12, Lost: 4, Drawn: 5

See Pantheon Players section for full details.

HENDRIE, Lee

Position: Attacking midfield.
Born: Birmingham, 18 May 1977
Career: ASTON VILLA (Youth Training Scheme, apprentice, June 1993, professional, May 1994); Stoke (loan, September 2006–May 2007); Sheffield United (free, July 2007–September 2009); Leicester (loan, February 2008–April 2008); Blackpool (loan, November 2008–January 2009); Derby (swap, September 2009–June 2010); Brighton (loan, March 2010–June 2010), Bradford City (August 2010–December 2010)

England

Caps: 1, Won: 1, Lost: 0, Drawn: 0, Goals: 0

Lee Hendrie's football ability was undoubted, but he was an underachiever. Whatever the final reckoning for a career which is still not yet ended, there can be no doubt about Lee Hendrie's skill level. He was capped at Youth, Under-21 and B team levels and was on course for a glittering career at the highest level. This was the season he shared the Midland Football Writers' Young

Player of the Year Award 1998–99 after playing his 50th game for the club. He was then 22. However, while Robbie Keane's career continued to rise, and in early 2011 he still plays in the Premiership with West Ham, Lee was scrapping for short-term contracts in the lower divisions.

Lee had access to plenty of advice on the issues facing a footballer, since his father played for Birmingham City, while cousin John had a professional career which took in Coventry, Newcastle, Bradford and Leeds. However, as Tony Matthews says in his *Villa Encylopaedia*, 'Lee can be a little hot headed at times'. Indeed so. Lee is one of the very few professional footballers ever to be sent-off in their first-team debut. Hendrie went on as substitute after 33 minutes for Mark Draper at QPR in December 2005, but was sent off in stoppage time for a second bookable offence.

Though Lee played enough games to be a member of the 300 club, he never shook off the image of being impetuous to the point of rashness. He did not impress Martin O'Neill when he became manager, and was sent out to Stoke then a Championship side, on loan, and then transferred to Sheffield United and his downward slide began, far too early to be satisfactory.

His England career consisted of one cap, as one of a Villa trio who played against the Czechs in a friendly on 18 November 1998, Paul Merson and Dion Dublin being the other two. Paul was completing a glittering career as an attacking midfield player and Lee Hendrie could have taken over from him as an ideal replacement in midfield. Indeed, when Merson was substituted for Hendrie on 77 minutes it might have seen the young pretender was taking over. However, this was to be his only cap. This was the high point of a career which failed to fulfil its promise.

HESKEY, Emile William Ivanhoe

Position: Striker
Born: Leicester, 11 January 1978
Career: Leicester City (1994–2000); Liverpool (£11 million, 2000–04); Birmingham City (2004–06); Wigan Athletic (2006–09); ASTON VILLA (£3.5 million, January 2009–present)

England
Caps: 62, Won: 31, Lost: 12, Drawn: 19, Goals: 6

Emile Heskey is a footballer with all the physical qualities of a top-class striker, but is not a prolific goalscorer. However, he is highly valued for his work rate and ability to provide a constant threat to defenders. Football is a team game, and he benefits the team as a whole. Managers and fellow strikers think highly of him and, while his career has shown peaks and troughs, he was recruited to the Villa by manager Martin O'Neill after a spell at Wigan and was taken to the World Cup in South Africa in 2010 by England manager Fabio Capello.

Heskey was discovered as a promising youth player by Leicester City and graduated through their Academy under Martin O'Neill. He attended the FA School of Excellence at Lilleshall, where Jamie Carragher remembers him as 'a shy striker called Emile Heskey', a telling comment on his lack of assertion as a teenager. (*Carra* p.47). Shyness was not obvious on the pitch, and he made his first-team breakthrough in 1995, aged 17.

He won a League Cup medal in 1997 and formed a partnership with

Tony Cottee in season 1998–99 which O'Neill claimed kept Leicester in the top flight. He went on to win the League Cup again in 2000. He was considered to have massive potential, and at the end of that season Liverpool signed him for a then club-record fee of £11 million. He was held in high regard by Under-21 manager Peter Taylor and, more importantly, by Liverpool striker Michael Owen, who welcomed the space he created for strikers like himself and Robbie Fowler.

He rose to a peak with a 23-goal haul in season 2000–01. This was not repeated, but then Liverpool manager Gerard Houllier made the claim his place was justified by 'how many goals we have scored that he has been involved in', a widely accepted view. The England management certainly agreed, as he won four caps in 1999, seven in 2000, nine in 2001, 11 in 2002, seven in 2003 and two in 2004. But by then, his Liverpool career had crashed. At the end of the 2003–04 season, Liverpool transferred him to Birmingham for £3.5 million, rising to £6.75 million over time. And at around the same time, 13 June 2004, his England career temporarily stalled. England were beaten 1–2 in the European Finals Championship Group match against France in Lisbon. Heskey had come on as a substitute for Rooney and was blamed for giving away the free-kick from which France equalised.

Again he did well for a time. In his first season 2004–05 Birmingham fans voted him Player of the Season, and he won most of the Man of the Match Awards. The next season he scored four goals in 34 appearances as the club were relegated and was criticised by the same City fans. On relegation he was transferred to Wigan, to stay in the Premiership for £5.5 million. He scored eight goals in 36 appearances, then in the 2007–08 season scored four goals in 28 appearances.

Nevertheless, he returned to the England side in September 2007 against Israel and Russia in European Qualifying matches. Eriksson replacement Steve McLaren recalled him and played him for the whole of both games but then dropped him, despite two 3–0 victories, both in September 2007. It is said McLaren recalled him because Michael Owen wanted to play with him, having valued his work at Liverpool. He certainly made an assist for Owen in the second game, receiving praise for his performance in both games.

Fabio Capello was an admirer of Heskey, calling him into the squad and playing him as substitute in the second half of a friendly against the Czechs on 20 August 2008. He played in four following World Cup Qualifiers through to the end of 2008, and it was as an established England player that he was transferred from Wigan to Villa in January 2009.

The Villa Era

Heskey played his first Villa game against Pompey on 27 January 2010, scoring the only goal. As a Villa player in 2009 Heskey played seven games for England, scoring two goals: England won four, lost two and drew one. On closer examination, it is clear Capello was not sure about Heskey compared to the rangy Peter Crouch or the speedy Defoe – or even Carlton Cole. In a 0–2 defeat by Spain Heskey only played the first half being replaced by Crouch. Against Slovakia on 28 March he scored but then went off injured after 15 minutes. He did better against Kazakhstan on 6 June scoring and winning a penalty in a 4–0 victory before being replaced by Defoe after 81 minutes. Capello seemed to favour Defoe against Heskey against Holland on 12 August he played only the first half before Defoe replaced him with an equaliser Heskey had not looked like scoring. The next three games he started then was replaced by Defoe, until on 10 October he was replaced by Carlton Cole.

He appeared to have lost his chance of going to the World Cup in South Africa, as he missed the next four internationals, but he was on the plane for the June 2010 competition – and as first-choice centre-forward. In the first match against USA he was substituted for Crouch on 79 minutes. On 18 June he started against Algeria, but on 74 minutes, having not scored, he was replaced by Jermaine Defoe. Defoe started, then on 86 minutes Heskey replaced him. It was a bizarre decision. Heskey has never been an impact player: he does not turn matches. But the same decision was made in Germany's decisive match on 27 June, when England were knocked out of the competition. With England 4–0 down, he was called into action after 71 minutes, and not suprisingly failed to score. He is not a miracle worker. It was a sad end to an honourable England career.

The Heskey Debate

At the heart of the debate is Heskeys' strike record, against his undoubted contribution to the effectiveness of the teams he plays for. The strike record is easy to examine. His overall contribution is less easy to assess, though he has influential supporters and statistics which suggest that overall goalscoring is not the full picture. One report said England scored once every 40 minutes when he did not play – but once every 20 with him on the pitch. He made a contribution not measured by his goal record (see table below).

Years	Team	Appearances/goals	%
1994–2000	Leicester City	154 (40)	26
2000–04	Liverpool	150 (39)	26
2004–06	Birmingham City	68 (14)	21
2006–09	Wigan Athletic	82 (15)	18.3
2009–10	Aston Villa	56 (7)	12.5

By the end of the 2009–10 season Heskey had made 37 starts for Villa, with 19 substitute appearances, and scored seven goals. Not a prolific record and perhaps the reason Villa broke its transfer record for Darren Bent. Goals scored are, however, not the full picture, as Michael Owen, Wayne Rooney and others were said to value Heskey's assists to goals scored by other players. There is good reason why Fabio Cappello reinstated Emile to the England squad – they score more goals when he is playing. The debate on Emile Heskey's record will continue.

Emile Heskey retired from England duty on 15 July 2010 after returning from England's unsuccessful World Cup campaign. He gained 62 caps and scored seven goals. He said 'I have enjoyed every moment of my England career and worn the shirt with pride'. There is no doubt he worked his shift and played for England to the best of his ability.

HITCHENS, Gerry (Gerald Archibald)

Position: Centre-forward
Born: Rawnsley, Staffordshire, 8 October 1934
Died: Wrexham, North Wales, 13 April 1983
Career: Kidderminster Harriers (August 1953); Cardiff City (£1,500, January 1955); ASTON VILLA (£22,500, December 1957); Inter Milan (£60,000, June 1961); Torino (£50,000, November 1962); Atalanta Bergamo (£25,000, June 1965); Cagliari, Sardinia (£5,000, June 1967); Worcester City (November 1969); Merthyr Tydfil (September 1971).
Hitchens retired in May 1972 and went into business in Pontypridd.

England
Caps: 7, Won: 4, Lost: 3, Drawn: 0, Goals: 5
See Pantheon Players section for full details.

HODGE, Steve (Stephen Brian)

Position: Left midfield
Born: Nottingham, 25 October 1962
Career: Nottingham Forest (apprentice, May 1978, professional, October 1980); ASTON VILLA (£450,000, August 1985); Tottenham Hotspur (£650,00, December 1986); Nottingham Forest (£575,000, August 1988); Leeds United (£900,000, July 1991); Derby (loan, August 1994); QPR (£300,000, October 1994); Watford (free transfer, February 1995); Hong Kong (January 1996); Leyton Orient (August 1997–May 1998); Notts County Academy Coach 2000–01)

England
Caps: 24, Won: 15, Lost: 4, Drawn: 5, Goals: 0

Steve Hodge was a highly successful midfield player who gained 24 caps with three different clubs, the first 11 with Aston Villa. He deserves to be remembered as the first Villa player to play in a World Cup Finals, in 1986. Four years earlier Peter Withe had been taken to Spain 82, but had not played. Alas Hodge is best remembered for an unwitting part in one of the great scandals of World Cup History, Maradonna's Hand of God goal in the Mexico World Cup. to eliminate England from the competition. It was Hodge's mistake which played the Argentinian onside.

He made his international reputation playing for Villa after spending five years at Nottingham Forest, something which is often forgotten – James Corbett writes that for the World Cup 'making the step up was Nottingham Forest's Steve Hodge...' (*England Expects*, p.371),

an astonishing mistake given that Hodge had been playing in the Villa set up since the summer of 1985 – and had won no caps until coming to the Villa.

Hodge was in fact bought by Graham Turner to replace Gordon Cowans, who was transferred to Bari in Italy's Serie A in summer 1985. Hodge would shadow Cowans at England level too, eventually supplanting Cowans. Hodge was seen as shadowing the injury prone Brian Robson. Robson dislocated his shoulder frequently, and manager Bobby Robson was seeking a reliable player to cover for him. He tried Gordon Cowans but he did not get the nod, and on the 26 March 1986 after a period of impressive form for the Villa, Hodge stepped up against the USSR by Steve Hodge. He was going to be on the plane for Mexico.

After playing two full games which convinced Bobby Robson he was international class, Hodge gained his fourth cap as the substitute for Bryan Robson, substituted for him again after 41 minutes in the second Mexico game, and was then played for all of the next three rounds of the competition. It was in gaining his eighth cap in the game against Argentina on 22 June that he became internationally famous. Five minutes into the second half, the world-class Maradonna ran at the England defence, tried to play a one-two but was intercepted by Hodge. However Hodge then sliced his clearance, which spun back into the England penalty area. Shilton came out to clear, decided to punch but was one on one with Maradonna who ran at him and quite illegally flicked the ball into the undefended net with his left hand. Amazingly, the goal stood and England were out of the competition.

No one could really blame Steve Hodge for this, and in the 1986–87 season he remained established in the England midfield, an ever present under Bobby Robson. But he would not be a Villa player much longer. Graham Turner was sacked in the close season, Hodge made a transfer request, and in December 1986 a big money offer from David Pleat's Tottenham led him to move to London. He had gained 11 caps while playing for Villa, and would gain another 13 for Spurs and Nottingham Forest. He played 70 games in a season and a half for Villa, scoring 16 times. He was an excellent midfield general and deserves to be remembered for more than playing Maradonna on-side in the Hand of God incident.

HODGETTS, Dennis

Position: Outside-left
Born: Birmingham, 20 November 1863
Died: Birmingham, 26 March 1945

Career: Birmingham St George's (1882); ASTON VILLA (February 1886); Small Heath (August 1896–August 1898); ASTON VILLA (youth-team coach, August 1898).

England
Caps: 6, Won: 5, Lost: 0, Drawn: 1

One of the great heroes of the club when it was making the transition from being a local community club to a professional outfit, Hodgetts was massively respected and was held in very high regard long after his playing career was over. He become a club vice-president and held this honorary position until his death in 1945. He was admired by supporters who could not have remembered him playing but who recognised his superb service for the club.

Hodgetts was always a whole-hearted player, turning out for 215 first-class matches and scoring 91 goals – not a bad haul for a winger – over 12 and a half years. He won two Division One Championships, 1894 and 1896, appeared in three FA Cup Finals, gaining winners' medals in 1887 and 1895, and had genuine star quality. He always turned out with immaculately parted hair and waxed moustache but proved no fancy Dan when the action started. His ball distribution was exceptional and he had the strength to be difficult to dispossess when the ball was at his feet. He had a powerful shot, just the qualities required to become a cult hero for the fans. The *Villa News* noted a decade after he had retired from the first team that 'at inside-left he made left-wingers play' (17 April 1908).

His England record was good. At a time when England only played three games per season his tally of six – all three in 1888, and recalls in 1892 and 1894 – was satisfactory, and the fact that he was never on the losing side impressive. *The Sporting Mail* noted of him in 1906, 'When he and Harry Wood played together, England had the best left-wing pair that has ever represented her'. The competition may have been more limited than today, but players can only rise above their contemporaries. Hodgetts certainly did.

Hodgetts occupies a unique place in the history of English – and so world – football in that he was the first player

to be sent off, and subsequently suspended, in a League match. This happened on 22 September 1888. Hodgetts was accused of punching the Everton defender, Alec Dick.

Villa News & Record 1, 1 September 1906
'A born football player. Remarkably clever with his feet, and possessed many original ideas. Effective in combination, an admirable coach, his skill and unselfishness having the happiest result. Shone especially in "nursing" players lighter and less skilful than himself, many juniors coming into prominence on the strength of his tuition and example.'

HOUGHTON, William Eric

Position: Left wing
Born: Billingborough, Lincolnshire, 29 June 1910
Died: Sutton Coldfield, 1 May 1996
Career: Donington School; Boston Town (1925); Billingborough FC (1926); ASTON VILLA (triallist then professional, 1927); guested Coventry, Leicester, Notts Forest and County in World War Two; Notts County (player, December 1946, then manager, April 1949–August 1953); ASTON VILLA (manager 1953–November 1958), Notts Forest (chief scout, November 1958–November 1960); Rugby Town

(manager February 1961–March 1964); Walsall (scout, late 1965, then director), ASTON VILLA (1970 as coach/assistant to Youth Development department, then director from September 1972, aged 62, to December 1979, aged 69, thereafter senior vice-president from January 1983 to his death in 1996)

Also played cricket for Warwickshire and Lincolnshire.

England

Caps: 7, Won: 6, Lost: 1, Drawn: 0, Goals: 5

Eric Houghton is a legend not just because of his playing career in the interwar years, but because he is one of a select band of players to have returned after playing to manage the club. In the five years he was manager, September 1953 to November 1958, Villa scored their last FA Cup triumph. Alas, he could not stop the club's continued decline.

Like many of the players in the first 60 or 70 years of the club's history, Houghton came to the club through family. Initially it was his uncle and ex Villa player 'Cec' Harris who persuaded him to try to get into the club when he scored 88 goals for his school side. He was accepted and gave up his baker's job and sign for £3 per week in August 1927. (Houghton's personal account is in the FA year book 1978–79, pp. 72–75). He got into the League side in January 1930 aged nineteen and a half, and replaced Arthur Dorrell, for whom he was a direct swap at left wing, playing alongside the experienced Billy Walker. He only exceeded Dorrell's 390 games by two, but scored 170 goals compared to Dorrell's 65.

For a winger, his scoring record was exceptional – five in seven games for England, 350 in all competitions (including second and third-team games) for the Villa. His main physical asset apart from direct speedy play was an exceptionally strong shot. The West Brom and England 'keeper Harold Pearson later stated that he had 'the hardest shot I ever faced'.

In September 1930 he was picked for a Football League team to play the Irish League in Belfast. Houghton did well enough to be selected for the full England team that October, followed by a second Football League team game in November. Houghton's first two games for England against Ireland and Wales led to victories by 5–1 and 4–0 respectively, In May 1931 he travelled to France and Belgium, failed to score in a 5 2 defeat, but helped in a 4–1 victory against the Belgians in which he scored again. His most successful game was his fifth, an away match to Ireland in Belfast where he scored twice in a 6–2 victory. He played in a 3–0 victory against the Scots in April 1932

and was picked to play alongside Billy Walker, who had been out of the England side for five years against the legendary Austrians.

Walker's appearance was controversial, Dixie Dean having been dropped along with the other four forwards. The selectors clearly wanted club players who had experience together. Meisl, the Austrian manager, had been so impressed by the difficulty of playing England at home that he had recruited Jimmy Hogan, the legendary English coach who was unable to get work at home. England scored twice, but could not prevent an Austrian goal.

When Houghton scored from a free kick, however, England should have been cruising. Instead, weaknesses in the long ball game which Hogan disliked allowed Austria to pin them back, and the final score of 4–3 flattered the English. Walker did not score, and while Houghton did, he never played again for England.

Houghton was a thoughtful player and, despite winning seven caps as a young player, realised there were limitations to the training methods at English clubs. Houghton noted in his memoir that every player on the staff at the Villa was given a book of the rules and ordered to study them. However, on the pitch the training was rudimentary and inadequate. He was impressed by the criticisms of Englishman Jimmy Hogan and the performance of the Austrians. He welcomed Hogan when he was appointed Villa's second manager in November 1936 – a controversial decision, particularly as Hogan was 54.

But it was not controversial to Eric Houghton. He wrote many years later 'I have often blessed the day I met Jimmy Hogan, who taught me so much about the game and about myself...Jimmy Hogan formulated what was to me the most successful Villa team of my time, though we were robbed of our just rewards by the intervention of World War Two'.

He managed Notts County after the war, but his real love was the Villa, and it seemed a marriage made in heaven when he returned as manager. His first act was to employ the legendary Hogan as youth coach and scout. But Hogan was in his seventies, too old to make a difference. Sadly the 1950s were the decade when Villa really began to slide, and the FA Cup win in 1957 was against the tide. A year later he was sacked.

But Houghton never really left the club. In the rebirth of club following the bankruptcy of the late 1960s, he returned in 1970 to help with youth development although 60. Two years later he retired from active duty and was made director then senior vice president. He held this last position at his death. He is a member of the 300 club.

JAMES, David Benjamin

Position: Goalkeeper
Born: Welwyn Garden City, 1 August 1970
Career: Watford (YTS, June 1986, professional, July 1988); Liverpool (£1 million, July 1992); ASTON VILLA (£1.8 million, June 1999); West Ham United (£3.5 million, July 2001); Manchester City (£2 million, January 2004–06); Portsmouth (£1.2 million, August 2006–10); Bristol City (free transfer, August 2010–present) England career ended with defeat in World Cup against Germany, 27 June 2010.

England

Caps: 53, Won: 29, Lost: 13, Drawn: 11, Goals: 0
While at Villa – three caps in 2001.

When manager John Gregory recruited David James to replace Mark Bosnich, who had taken a freedom of contract opportunity to leave Villa thinking the grass was greener at Manchester United, James was already an established and experienced goalkeeper.

James played two seasons for the Villa, in season 1999–2000 taking part in a roller coaster ride with an awful first half raising the prospect of relegation, culminating in a dreadful match against relegation rivals Sheffield Wednesday in which Dion Dublin broke his neck – and then a recovery which took Villa to Wembley for the FA Cup and sixth place in the Premiership. James did not win any caps in this season, though he played a key part in the third best defence in the division, conceding only 35 goals in a 20 club division. The next season saw the defence less secure, conceding 43 goals, making them joint sixth in the division, and he moved to West Ham.

His Villa performances brought him back into England contention, and in the 2000–01 season he won a cap against Italy in a 1–0 defeat on 15 November 2000 after a three-and-a-half-year absence. He won two more caps as a Villa player, in February 2001 against Spain and May of the same year against Mexico. Both games were won with James keeping clean sheets, and as the game against

Spain took place at Villa Park, James joined the select band of Villains who have won caps on their own home ground. James never again dropped out of England contention for long. Playing for Villa rescued his England career.

Alas, while his ability as a shot stopper was undeniable, his tendency to make bizarre mistakes, often due to a lack of concentration, had given him the name 'Calamity James'. This improved with experience and while he never fulfilled his immense potential while at the Villa, the experience put him back into the frame for the England job. He outlived many younger goalies and Capello as England manager kept faith with him in the 2010 World Cup. He replaced Green of West Ham after a howler as bad as anything James had ever done in the first match. Alas, it is almost certain the German victory in South Africa ended his England career.

KIRTON, William John

Position: Inside-forward
Born: Newcastle upon Tyne, 2 December 1896
Died: Sutton Coldfield, 27 September 1970
Career: Pandon Temperance FC (1917); Leeds City (May 1919); ASTON VILLA (£500, October 1919); Coventry City (September 1928); Kidderminster Harriers (September–October 1930);

Leamington Town (November 1930–July 1931)
Kirton later ran a newsagents in Kingstanding, Birmingham.

England
Caps: 1, Won: 0, Lost: 0, Drawn: 1, Goals: 1

Kirton came to Villa along with Clem Stephenson's younger brother, George, in the auction of assets of Leeds City following their expulsion from the League in 1919. Kirton was priced at £500 and Stephenson £250, both ludicrously low fees for players who would play for England – though

George Stephenson did so after leaving Villa and is not featured in this book. Aged 23 when he joined Villa, Billy Kirton spent his prime footballing years at Villa Park, playing alongside fine players like Billy Walker, Clem Stephenson, and Dicky York. In nine years he played 261 first-class games, scoring 59 times and gaining a Cup-winners' medal in 1920 and a losers' medal in 1924. He left when aged 28 as part of the rebuilding which took place after Rinder was removed from the board.

Kirton played only one game for England, against Ireland on 22 November 1921, and though he scored the equalising goal he never played for the country again. There is very little information about Kirton, and despite being a regular for his club he was one of the players who manages to leave very little information on a successful career.

LEAKE, Alexander

Position: Defender
Born: Small Heath, Birmingham, 11 July 1871
Died: Birmingham, 29 March 1938
Career: Hoskins and Sewell FC; Kings Heath Albion; Saltley Gas Works FC; Singers, Hoskins and Sewell; Old Hill Wanderers; Small Heath Alliance (July 1894); ASTON VILLA (June 1902); Burnley (December 1907–May 1910); Wednesbury Old Athletic (July 1910–May 1912); Crystal Palace

(trainer-coach, July 1912–May 1915); Merthyr Tydfil (trainer-coach, October 1919–July 1920); Walsall (trainer, (September 1932–May 1933).

England

Caps: 5, Won: 4, Lost: 0, Drawn: 1

Alexander Leake is one of the mystery players of the Villa's golden period, firstly because he was a late developer, coming to Villa when he was over 30 from Small Heath (now Birmingham City), where he played 221 games for the Blues in eight years, the last six as captain. Moving to a bigger club and playing at a higher level at the age of 31 is unusual. Playing for over five years,

totalling 140 senior games, and winning an FA Cup-winners' medal (in 1905, when he was nearly 34) is remarkable. Yet Leake's unusual career did not provoke much comment and he is an obscure figure.

We know that Leake reached his peak at the time of the 1905 Cup Final because he won his five caps for England in the period just before the match. In 1904 he was called up for the Ireland game (12 March) and played the next game against Scotland in April. He must have impressed, because he played all three home internationals in 1905, the year of his Cup Final medal. Despite this, there is little information on his feats and nothing to indicate how this defender managed to have such a long career.

Not breaking into League soccer until he was nearly 24 must have had something to do with it, but the impression given by the reports is of a solid, hard-working full-back, not an international-quality player, which cannot be right. Reports dwell on his honesty, good humour and his ability to play party tricks with a ball. All of this is fine, but they do not paint a portrait of a player with five years' experience at the top level of English soccer. The *Villa News* comment sounds like a teacher on a rather moderate pupil. Leake remains a mystery.

Villa News & Record 1, 1 September 1906

A good tempered, honest worker: safe rather than showy. Hard to beat in a tackle, and good at spoiling an opponent's pass. Alert, keeps his head, and never tires in the hardest of matches. His unfailing good humour has made him a general favourite.

LITTLE, Brian

Position: Inside-forward
Born: 25 November 1953, Newcastle upon Tyne*
Career: Trial with Burnley, Leeds United, Manchester City, Newcastle United, Stoke City, Sunderland and West Bromwich Albion (August 1968–May 1969); ASTON VILLA (trial then apprentice, July 1969, professional, June 1971). Playing career ended 10 March 1980.
Left Villa May 1982 after working briefly in the offices of the club's Development Association.
*Though most of the books and the FA say Peterlee, County Durham, this is Brian's own stated birthplace.

Brian then had a second career in management, leading to him coming back to Villa as manager and winning silverware. This career ran: ASTON VILLA (coach, season 1985–86); Wolverhampton Wanderers (coach January 1986, caretaker manager August–October 1986); Middlesbrough (coach); Darlington (manager, February 1989–May 1991); Leicester City (manager, May 1991–November 1994); ASTON VILLA (manager, November 1994–February 1998); Stoke City (manager, May 1998–August 1999); West Bromwich Albion (manager, May 1999–March 2000); Hull City (manager, August 2000–February 2002); Sky Sport soccer reporter and summariser (season 2002–03); Tranmere Rovers (manager, October 2003–June 2006); Wrexham (November 2007–September 2008); Gainsborough Trinity (manager, September 2008–present).

England

Caps: 1, Won: 0, Lost: 0, Drawn: 1

Brian Little became a legend at Villa Park, and Leon Hickman is among many fans who watched the Villa in the 1970s for whom Brian was the most-loved player of the period. Though a member of the 300 club with 302 appearances and 82 goals his career was hit by injury and sadly cut short at 27. He played so many games because he started so young, playing his first senior game when only 18. At his peak he was a scintillating player whose legend powerfully contributed to his being called back to be manager in the 90s. But in hindsight, the Brian Little story is one of promise unfulfilled rather than achievement.

Brian joined Villa at age 15. He was one of two outstanding players from the 1972 FA Youth Cup-winning side (the other was John Gidman), a team which won the Dusseldorf International Youth Tournament that year. He made his first-team breakthrough in the same year, playing in the match against Torquay on 29 April 1972 which clinched the Third Division title. Little scored once and set up two goals in a 5–1 victory and it was clear Villa had an outstanding young forward prospect on the books. In 1972–73 he established himself as an inside-forward alongside Andy Lochhead, kept his place when Sammy Morgan replaced Lochhead at centre-forward, and then when Andy Gray came down from Scotland as the most dynamic centre-forward Villa had seen for years, partnered him in an exceptionally promising forward line. Villa veteran Charlie Aitken who played in the same team said 'Brian Little was a world-class player. He was brilliant at running across the back four. He'd watch your foot come back then go with perfect timing'. (McColl p.84)

Brian was the first Villa player to be capped since Gerry Hitchens, and the first since Villa's return to the First Division under Ron Saunders (John Gidman was the second, two years later). Sadly after his England debut, sent on as a substitute against Wales

on 21 May 1975, he suffered an injury hit season in 1975–76, Villa's first back in the top flight, and while he appeared to have fully recovered and played scintillating football for the Villa, he was never capped again. Perhaps he suffered from Villa's lack of glamour under Saunders, who at this point had only the 1975 League Cup victory to show for his managerial skills. When Brian was selected for the squad Villa were clearly on the up, but without the credibility of more established sides. The week after Little's one appearance, England won 5–1

against Scotland at Hampden, so an untested player seemed irrelevant.

In nine years as a professional at Villa, he only played four seasons without injury, and so his career rarely developed momentum. In a total of 82 goals in 302 games, 69 came in 192 matches. He twice won League Cup medals, in 1975 and 1977, peak seasons for Little's game with in the latter season the Little-Gray partnership scoring 29 goals – 11 for Brian. But in the 1977–78 season despite a fine UEFA Cup run ended by Johan Cruyff's Barcelona, the team fell apart. Gidman and Gray clashed with Saunders – the Little-Gray partnership only scoring 11 altogether as both struggled with knee injuries. Gray left and Little was never as effective. On 10 March 1980 he suffered a catastrophic knee injury and his career was finished at 27.

Without the injuries, had he played more football in the First Division, Brian Little may well have become a major England player. England managers simply would not take a chance on a player they saw as injury prone. However, at Villa Park he was a hero, and was given the chance to come back as manager after leaving Leicester City. He replaced Ron Atkinson after Doug Ellis sacked a flambouyant but failing manager for a less high-profile appointment. Curiously, both men had been on Villa's books, though Atkinson never

played for the first team. Little built a successful side – for a time.

He won the League Cup as a manager this time, in 1996, before again seeing a Villa team fall apart. The sense of potential never fulfilled came back to haunt him and John Gregory was called in to haul the team away from relegation, causing Little to resign. But no manager since Brian Little has delivered a trophy.

Leon Hickman on Brian Little:
'When the claret-and-blue manager in the sky names the club's greatest eleven, he will risk the unbridled wrath of those of us who followed Villa in the seventies if Britain Little is omitted from the list. His playing career harrowingly cut short at 27, Little still registers the highest marks for ball-control, style and an unconquerable belief that football was the thing.' *Villa Greats*, p.84.

LOWE, Edmund (Eddie)

Position: Defender
Born: Halesowen, 11 July 1925
Died: 9 March 2009
Career: Millwall, amateur (1940), Napier Aircraft Company, Finchley; Kynoch Works XI; ASTON VILLA (May 1945); Fulham (£15,000, with brother Reg, May 1950); Notts County (player-manager, July 1963–April 1965).

Lowe became a purchasing manager for a Nottingham boiler and central heating company after his retirement.

England

Caps: 3, Won: 2, Lost: 1, Drawn: 0

Under the tuition of manager Alex Massie, Eddie Lowe became Villa's first post-war international. He was part of the new group of players who would have to take the club forward after six years of conflict and played in the Villa's first post-war match in August 1946. A local boy from Halesowen, he was quickly recognised as having talent and could have been a half-back in the Massie mould. He was picked as reserve for the England versus Scotland game in April 1947, aged only 21 and

in his first season of professional football. He then played in three internationals in May 1947, after only playing in one full season after the war, helping achieve victory against France, a surprising loss against Switzerland, and a 10–0 defeat of Portugal, all away from home. After three caps, however, his career stagnated.

The writer Peter Morris, who saw him play, wrote that he was not able to develop his talent because the Villa crowd wanted strong, hard men to save the club from relegation. This is possibly true, but if so it was a very short-sighted policy. Lowe and his brother soon left to play for Fulham, a less successful club but one which gave them security. This saga suggests that, as Danny Blanchflower and Tommy Thompson were to discover a few years later, Villa were no longer the 'soccer university' they had been previously and would struggle to produce internationals in the post-war era.

Going to Fulham was, however, a step down. Villa were certainly struggling – in the first four seasons after they were eighth, sixth, 10th and 12th in the old Division One. Fulham had spent the first three years in Division Two but were promoted in 1948–49. The club struggled towards the bottom of the Division, and the Lowe brothers were signed to bolster their fortunes. This did not happen, and in the season 1951–52 they were relegated back to Division Two. That year Villa leaped from 15th to sixth in Division One. Perhaps Lowe regretted leaving Villa Park, but the bridges had been burned. Lowe was certainly never able to develop the talent that he had showed in that first season of 1946–47, and it was Villa's loss as well as his own.

Peter Morris on Edmund Lowe in *Aston Villa: The History of a Great Football Club, 1874–1960*:

'The trouble was that the Villa crowd in the ever-anxious winters between 1946 and 1950 had no time for players of Eddie Lowe's type. They wanted the heavy stuff – stuff they believed would get the Villa out of relegation trouble. Strong-arm men were "in" and class ball-players like Lowe, and managers like Massie, who preached football instead of "thump", were "out". Eventually Massie went. A little later Eddie Lowe and his brother Reg followed suit to do Fulham and themselves proud.' (Peter Morris, *Aston Villa: The History of a Great Football Club, 1874–1960*, 1960, p.193)

MERSON, Paul Charles

Position: Attacking midfielder
Born: Harlesden, London 20 March 1968
Career: Arsenal (Schoolboy forms, April 1982, apprentice, July 1984,

professional, December 1985–July 1997), Brentford (loan, January–May 1987), Middlesbrough (£4.5 million, July 1997), VILLA (£6.75 million, September 1998), Portsmouth (free, July 2002), Walsall (free, July 2003). Caretaker manager March 2004, player-manager May 2004–February 2006. Tamworth February–May 2006 (one game). Currently a TV sports commentator.

England
Caps: 21, Won: 5, Lost: 7, Drawn: 9, Goals: 3

A brilliantly gifted midfield attacker, flexible, athletic and with an excellent work ethic, Paul Merson spent most of his career and won most of his caps with Arsenal, but in nearly three and half years at Villa won the respect of the fans for his talent and whole hearted commitment to the cause. He had already played over 500 games when he arrived at Villa Park, and was to win the last of his caps shortly after his arrival, but he had not come to wind down. His commitment was always excellent.

His skills were never in doubt. He was voted PFA Young Player of the Year in 1989, aged 21. But through his career he fought a battle against addiction, made public in November 2004. As time went on this dominated the headlines. When his off field problems overwhelmed him he had to take time off for the game, and spent time in a hospital for addictive illnesses before the France 98 World Cup Finals. His footballing recovery was, however, complete, and when he played his problems were left behind. He was transferred to Middlesbrough in 1997 for what was then a record fee for a non-Premier club but did not settle and his transfer to Villa happened shortly afterward in September 1998.

His England career was coming to an end, and some felt that the £6.75 million fee Villa paid for him by John Gregory was excessive for a 30-year-old player. But Merson was well respected by the Villa fans who welcomed his commitment and determination, and understood his off field battle with drink, drugs and gambling. After winning a cap on 18 November 1998 he retired from international football and this allowed him to concentrate on League form, which was something of a roller coaster. He played a crucial role in the fight against relegation at the end of 1999, notably in a memorable game against Sheffield Wednesday on 18 December.

Villa approached Christmas failing badly and played a Wednesday side dropping like a stone in a six-pointer. For the first hour, Villa lost the plot and their centre-forward – this was the game where Dublin broke his neck. All players, including Merson, were awful, and when he missed a penalty with Wednesday leading 0–1 the atmosphere was dreadful. With the pundits speculating the manager was half an hour from the sack, Merson rolled his sleeves up and with midfield dynamo Ian Taylor took the game to Wednesday. The two men tore apart the opposition, both scored to win the game, and turned the season around. Five months later Villa were at Wembley in the FA Cup. Merson had lifted the whole squad.

Paul Merson could be compared to both Paul Gascoigne and David Platt. On the field Merson had a similar attacking flair and work ethic as Platt, though scoring fewer goals

(19 in 144 appearances, while Platt scored 68 in 155). But off the field, he was as different from the model professional Platt as could be imagined, as their two autobiographies show. He shared many of the same personal problems as Gazza, with whom he once shared a house. But he was far less deeply troubled than Gascoigne, and faced up to the problems in a manner, winning respect. His autobiography is sometimes harrowing, but always engaging. Merson had lost some of the pace he had had with Arsenal in his medal-winning days, but his role was memorable particularly in the season of 1999–2000 when he played in the losing FA Cup team and won the supporters' and player's trophies for Villa Player of the Year. It remains a mystery why, when many thought he had more to give, Graham Taylor in his second spell as manager allowed him to go on a free transfer to Portsmouth.

MILNER, James

Born: Leeds, 4 January 1986
Career: Leeds United (debut as substitute 2002, aged 16 years and 309 days); Newcastle United (2004); ASTON VILLA (loanee for one year, 2005–06); Newcastle (2006); ASTON VILLA (£12 million, August 2008); Manchester City (18 August 2010–present)

England

Caps: 9, Won: 1, Lost: 4, Drawn: 4
Caps with Villa: 12.

James Milner had an unusually long rise to the top, particularly as he started young. He joined the Academy of his local team, Leeds United, at 10 years old and became both a youthful prodigy while being something of a late developer. He was the second-youngest player in Premiership history playing for Leeds on 10 November 2002 when not yet 17.

However, he was caught up in the turmoil at Leeds and was transferred to Newcastle United in July 2004. Newcastle was as turbulent as Leeds, and he was loaned to David O'Leary's

Aston Villa. He was a successful winger and was nearly signed by Martin O'Neill but at the last moment was recalled to Newcastle. Constant managerial and club changes were not ideal for his development, but he was outwardly undisturbed and applied himself with a superb work ethic. But in the summer of 2008 he put in a written transfer request away from St James' Park. On 29 August 2008 he came back to Villa Park.

Initially played as a wing player, in the 2009–10 season he was moved into midfield with great success. His form at Villa earned him a call up for the England first team by Fabio Capello on 7 February 2009. He stated that his time at the Villa was the 'most settled' period of his career, having had 13 managers and caretaker managers despite being only 23. Perhaps this was a reason why his international career stalled at Under-21 level.

He played virtually every game for the Under-21s for five years and must have been profoundly frustrated at not making the breakthrough to the full team. As the *Guardian* said when he gained his first cap, 'He must have been disappointed to be stuck in the England Under-21 squad for so long that he set the record for his country with 46 appearances'. (2 September 2009). But Milner never showed resentment, and he displayed a readiness to buckle down and do what was required, which is to his credit. It is not suprising that Villa wanted him on their books not once but twice.

Milner played 46 games for the Under-21 team, not only a record for England but equalling the European record for Under-21 caps, shared with Pirlo, an Italian player. This is a remarkable record, even more so because he did not start with the Under-21s particularly young – while his Premiership career began as a prodigy; he was 18 when he gained his first Under-21 cap on 30 March 2004.

However, his move to Villa kick-started his progress. Milner was called up for the full squad in February 2009 but he did not get to play. His first appearance for England was in the Holland friendly in Amsterdam on 12 August 2009, replacing Ashley Young for the last 23 minutes. He made an immediate impact on the left wing, outrunning the Dutch defender and crossing into the six-yard box for Defoe to score the equaliser. He had shown his quality.

While at Villa he became established in the England team, and by the time of the World Cup of 2010 he played in three of the four games. Substituted in the first game suffering from a stomach upset, he missed the second game but played in the final two. Sadly, he was part of the team which went out to Germany. He played one more game for England while at Villa before being transferred for £26 million.

MORLEY, William Anthony ('Tony')

Position: Outside-left
Born: Ormskirk, 26 August 1954
Career: Preston North End, (apprentice, July 1969, professional, August 1972); Burnley (£100,000, February 1976); ASTON VILLA (£200,000, June 1979); West Bromwich Albion (£75,000, December 1983); Birmingham City (loan, November–December 1984); FC Seiko, Japan (August 1985); FC Den Haag, Holland (July 1986); Walsall, trial (June 1987); West Bromwich Albion (August 1987); Burnley (loan, October–November 1988); Tampa Bay Rowdies, USA (March 1989); Hamrun Spartans, Malta (April 1990); New Zealand Football (1990–91); Sutton Coldfield Town (1992); Bromsgrove Rovers (player-coach, January 1995); Stratford Town (1992); Bromsgrove Rovers (player-coach, January 1995); Stratford Town (player, March 1995).

England

Caps: 6, Won: 4, Lost: 0, Drawn: 2

Tony Morley was a pacey left-winger, crossing at speed and scoring with both feet. A goal against Everton at Goodison in February 1981 was voted Goal of the Season. In June 1979 Saunders began building his third side, and the second great one, as the 1977 League Cup-winning side was breaking up partly due to players falling out with the abrasive manager. Andy Gray, John Gidman, Gordon Smith, John Gregory and John Deehan all fell out and were transferred, while Brian Little wanted a transfer but was denied by a back injury. The fans wondered whether Saunders knew what he was doing.

Morley's arrival from Burnley for £200,000 initially appeared to be a mistake, as injury and loss of form dogged him in the 1979–80 season. Morley never fully accepted Saunders's demands for wingers to track back, but he toed the line and in his second season, 1980–81, his form was a revelation as Villa strode to the Championship. Few players have turned their fortunes around so completely. Gordon Cowans later commented: 'Tony, being the flair player that he was, I think it took longer for him to come to terms with Ron Saunders and the way he wanted him to play…He didn't expect his wingers just to be waiting out on the wings for the ball to come to them. They were expected to get back and defend as well…That didn't come naturally to Tony…'

Gordon also testifies, 'He had fantastic ability. He was great going forward, had two great feet and was

a fine crosser of the ball. He came up with his fair share of goals as well, and they were usually spectacular. Tony was probably our match winner: on his day he could turn things round and create things for us'. (McColl p.99). This is true, as all those who saw him will testify. He was also a confidence player, and his away goal against Dynamo Berlin in the European Cup campaign of 1981–82 from a run inside his own half has been described as 'For style, individual determination and importance, the most outstanding goal in Villa's history' (McColl p.103). Its quality was vital for Morley himself. He had begun to struggle again and said after the match, 'Once I start getting goals I have the confidence to keep trying with shots from any range with either foot'.

Morley placed a decisive role in every game in the European Cup run, notably in the Final when Bayern had put a man on Morley to mark him out the game. It succeeded until the 67th minute, when Shaw whipped a pass behind two German defenders, including Morley's marker. In space for a brief moment, Morley turned the centre-half and whipped in a cross to Peter Withe. The ball bobbled, but Withe got a shin to it and scored the goal that won the European Cup. Morley had risen to the occasion.

Determination and skill forced England manager Ron Greenwood to call him up. In the run-up to the 1982 World Cup he and Peter Withe were both called up but hardly ever together. In only two of the six games he played did Morley and Withe repeat their successful Villa partnership. After two games without Withe, both were called up for the 1–0 victory over Wales on 27 April 1982, but they were then dropped. While both were recalled for the 1–1 draw against Iceland on 2 June 1982 they never played together again for England. Greenwood did not take either player to the World Cup in Spain. England did not get through the second round. Would Morley and Withe have made a difference?

New coach Bobby Robson picked Morley but not Withe for his first game on 22 September 1982. This was Morley's fifth cap, and finally, after a one-game absence, he was recalled for a three-goal victory against the Greeks on 17 November 1982. All Morley's caps came in the peak year of the European Cup victory when his confidence was at its highest.

While Morley did not play for England again, he played in the successful two-legged victory in the Super Cup of 1982 over Barcelona. When he was sold in the 1983–84 season it was for financial reasons and was clearly premature. Fans never really forgave Doug Ellis. Tony Morley has never been forgotten at Villa Park.

MORT, Thomas

Position: Full-back
Born: Kearsley, Bolton, 1 December 1897
Died: Wigan, 6 June 1967
Career: Altrincham (December 1918), previously Lancashire Fusiliers during World War One; Rochdale (June 1921); ASTON VILLA (April 1922–May 1935). Retired to go into business in Wigan.

England

Caps: 3, Won: 1, Lost: 2, Drawn: 0, Goals: 0

Mort was partner to Tommy Smart in a full-back partnership known as 'Death and Glory', Mort being the 'death' element. But both are obscure. Both men were outstandingly successful for Aston Villa, playing an immense number of games for the club and achieving great popularity. Yet there very little hard information about them. Mort is known as a master of the sliding tackle, but otherwise his style of defending is lost. For someone who played for the Villa over 13 years, played 368 senior matches and was one of the players in the 1924 FA Cup defeat – not much written about for obvious reasons – Mort is virtually unknown.

Equally suprising, given the success the partnership had for Villa, England only played the two players together once – in the Home Championship match against Wales on 3 March 1924. This was during an outstandingly successful season defensively for Villa, in which the team conceded only 37 goals in a 22-team division – by a mile the best defensive record Villa achieved in the interwar years. Mort and Smart were at the heart of the success, and with such a record and the Villa on the way to Wembley it is not suprising

they were chosen. But only once did England pick them together.

Though England lost that match 2–1, it is difficult to see why a successful club partnership could not be recreated at national level. Mort won only three caps, his partner only four. Smart had already won one in 1921, and logically bringing him back to play with Mort made sense. Yet the pairing was never repeated. Instead, Smart was chosen in April but not Mort, and Mort chosen in May, but not Smart. They were then both dropped till October 1925 when Smart got his final cap, and April 1926 when Mort gained his third and last England honour.

Logic does not explain this odd pattern, but the English selection committee was never particularly logical. Perhaps England was spoilt for choice where the full-back positions were concerned, and the Villa men were stop gaps, not top drawer? Defensively the Villa were not exceptional and in the late 1920s came to rely on all out attack. However, it was only the season after Mort retired that the defence conceded 110 goals and Villa were finally relegated. He and Smart had done a good job for Villa. Why they could not do the same for England is a mystery.

MOSS, Frank (Senior)

Position: Half-back/centre-half
Born: Aston, Birmingham, 17 April 1895
Died: Worcester, 15 September 1965
Career: Aston Manor; Walsall (August 1912); ASTON VILLA (February 1914); Cardiff City (£2,500, January 1929); Oldham Athletic (August 1929); Bromsgrove Rovers (player-manager 1930); Worcester City (1932). Retired in 1934 to continue as the licensee of the Grosvenor Arms, Worcester (1930–65).

England

Caps: 5, Won: 1, Lost: 1, Drawn: 3, Goals: 0

Frank Moss was a successful player in the era when Villa drew on men who were born and grew up in Aston, and remarkably the father of two sons who played for the Villa after World War Two. He was, however, one of the last players of the Rinder era, and his career a sign that Villa was starting to lose touch with a changing game. The fair-haired Frank 'Snowy' Moss signed from Walsall and seems to have played two games for the Villa in 1915 before the war closed down football. Reports that he made a 'fairy tale debut' for Villa in the 1920 FA Cup Final victory are wrong, though he did replace Jimmy Harrop at the 11th hour when Harrop was injured.

Moss led the defence at a time when Villa were still major players in the footballing world and a regular supplier of internationals. Nevertheless, they struggled to get higher than fifth in the First Division and only in the season Moss left did they reach the top three. They regularly conceded over 70 goals per season in a 22 club divison, and only in one season in the 1920s did they concede less than 50. Defensive weakness pointed to Villa falling behind tactically – the dominant sides of the period, Huddersfield and Arsenal, both managed by the genius who was Herbert Chapman, showed a committee was not the way to run a club. Villa were out of date in doing without a manager, and Moss was the an old type of centre-half made redundant by the change in the offside law in 1925.

His ability was, however, considerable, and over four years his caps showed he was respected – even if five was not a great haul. Like Mort and Smart, he seems to have been a stop gap, winning caps at intervals – October 1921, March and October 1922, November 1923 and April 1924. But there is no doubt he was respected. He captained both the Villa and England on successive Saturdays at Wembley in 1924, the first appearance being in the FA Cup victory along with Walker and Smart. Alas the Cup match was a defeat, underlining Villa's inability to win silverware, something which lasted for nearly 40 years. Villa's decline did not set in fully till the 1930s, but for Moss and his old-fashioned style of football the writing was on the wall.

OLNEY, Benjamin Albert

Position: Goalkeeper
Born: Holborn, London, 15 March 1899
Died: Derby, 23 September 1943
Career: Fairleys Athletic; Aston Park Rangers; Brierley Hill Alliance;

Stourbridge (August 1919); Derby County (£800, April 1921); ASTON VILLA (December 1927); Bilston United, player-manager (July 1930); Walsall (August 1931); Shrewsbury Town (August 1932); Moor Green, reinstated as an amateur (August 1933–April 1935).

England

Caps: 2, Won: 2, Lost: 0, Drawn: 0

The career of Ben Olney is mysterious. He played in the Second Division for Derby County for six seasons, including the promotion season of 1925–26, but after promotion lost his place to Harry Wilkes. Presumably Derby saw him as a competent Division Two goalkeeper

but not up to playing in Division One. According to Simon Betts, however (p.188), Villa were suffering from a goalkeeping crisis in the winter of 1926–27 and after suffering successive defeats over the Christmas period were willing to sign Derby's reserve 'keeper. Olney's remarkable turn of fortune was followed even more remarkably only four months later by winning two caps for England. Clearly, while Derby did not think he was up to the highest level Villa and the England selectors did. The reasons for this rapid rise remain difficult to trace to this day.

Douglas Lamming states that he was 'powerfully built, possessing fine anticipation and consistent to a degree' (p.187), but this says very little. He made 97 appearances for Villa in a reasonably successful period before being replaced by Fred Biddlestone in 1930. Why Villa had not signed him earlier is unknown – his family moved to the Black Country when he was 10. According to Lamming, after an impressive display for Birmingham FA in a 'junior international' against Scotland Olney was signed by Derby, which is odd. Why Derby when he was playing in the Black Country? What was a junior international at this period? He was, after all, 21 when signed. And if he played for Aston Park Rangers, was he on the doorstep of the Villa and missed by the scouts?

All that can be said definitely is that he played in goal for Villa sufficiently well to be picked twice for England, playing on 17 May 1928 in France in a 5–1 victory (he was beaten in the second minute but not again) and two days later in Antwerp against Belgium, again in a victory of 3–1. Conceding only two goals in two games, both won, is impressive, yet he never played for England again. He is also said to have played in two 'unofficial test matches' against South Africa in 1929, which are even more obscure. He is described as providing an 'efficient last line of defence'. Clearly he was a good goalkeeper but never quite convinced as the very top quality – despite a good international record. This would need Sherlock Holmes to explain.

Peter Morris has only one entry on Olney, noting that in the 1927–28 season Villa lost in the semi-final from a penalty which Olney partially stopped but went in off the underside of the bar , but has no more to say about him (Peter Morris, *Aston Villa: The history of a great football club, 1874–1960*, 1960, p.137).

PLATT, David Andrew

Position: Attacking midfield.
Born: Oldham, 10 June 1966
Career: South Chadderton Comprehensive School (Oldham); Boundary Park Juniors; Chadderton, amateur; Manchester United (apprentice, June 1982, professional, July 1984); Crewe Alexandra, (free transfer, February 1985); ASTON VILLA (£200,000, February 1988); Bari, Italy (£5.5 million, July 1991); Juventus, Italy (£6.5 million, June 1992); Sampdoria, Italy, (£5.25 million, August 1993); Arsenal (£4.75 million, July 1995); Sampdoria, Italy (free transfer, player-coach-manager, August–November 1998); Nottingham Forest (player-manager, August 1999–July 2001); England Under-21 (coach-manager, July 2001–May 2004).

See Pantheon section for full details.

REYNOLDS, John 'Baldy'

Position: Right-half/half-back
Born: Blackburn, 21 February 1869
Died: 12 March 1917
Career: Portglenone and Ballymena Schools (County Antrim, Ireland); Park Road FC, Blackburn; Witton FC; Blackburn Rovers reserves (1884–85); Park Road FC (1886); East Lancashire Regiment (December 1886, posted to Ireland); Distillery (1888); Ulster (June 1890); West Bromwich Albion (March 1891); Droitwich Town (guest, on loan, 1891–92); ASTON VILLA (£50, April 1893); Celtic (May 1897); Southampton St Marys (February 1898); Bristol St Georges (July 1898); Royston FC/Yorkshire (September

1899); New Zealand – Grafton FC (coach 1902–03); Stockport County (player August–October 1903); Willesden Town (January 1904, retired April 1905); Cardiff City (coach 1907–08). Moved to Sheffield on leaving Ninian Park and worked as a miner till his death at the age of only 48.

England

Caps: 8, Won: 5, Lost: 1, Drawn: 2, Goals: 3

Reynolds also played five times for Ireland before his English birth was discovered.

There is an air of mystery about John Reynolds which is hard to understand given his prominent career. The obvious mystery is how an Englishman came to be brought up in Ireland, then went to Blackburn – with a spell at a Witton FC which surely cannot have been in Birmingham – then up and down the country till arriving at Villa. Books disagree on when and where he moved, though all agree he played five times for Ireland at international level before discovering he could play for England and moving to a highly successful career at West Brom and Villa – with a break at Droitwich after he fell out with the Baggies committee – and finishing successfully at Glasgow Celtic. This is not the usual career pattern of a player in the Victorian period, but it is hard to explain what happened.

The ability of what some describe unflatteringly as this 'wee balding man' is however undeniable. He scored against Villa in the notorious Cup Final defeat to the Baggies in 1892 and when he left them under a cloud, Villa quickly signed him and his international record for two countries – virtually unique – speaks for itself.

For England he was on the losing side only once in eight games showing this was a strong team, and with six of his games against the stronger of England's three local rivals, Scotland. The fact he was on the winning side four times, drawing once and losing once attracted Celtic's attention. He was successful in three countries – Irish winners prize with Ulster in

1891, three English Cup-winners' medals – for Albion 1892, Villa 1895 and 1897, three League Championship medals, and then the Scottish Cup with Celtic in 1898. Apart from his caps, he also played for the Football League three times. This would be remarkable in any era, but with the limited opportunities for a Victorian footballer, it is truly astonishing. Reynolds only played 110 games for Villa, scoring 17 goals, and only 14 games were in the FA cup, the only competition apart from the League which was around at the time. He never scored in the FA Cup for Villa, yet in this limited number of appearances won two Cup-winners' medals.

John Reynolds, with his balding head and slight resemblance to Shakespeare, stares at the camera in the photos as an enigma that has never been solved. *The Complete Record* (2010 p.263) says 'his life and exploits are still the subject of lectures at the University of Ulster'. It is not at all suprising. He clearly made the most of his opportunities.

Villa News & Record 1, 1 September 1906
'A remarkably smart half-back. For his inches a perfect wonder. Knew every "trick of the trade" and usually showed up well in big matches. Had a happy knack of scoring at critical moments.'

Howard Spencer (captain Villa and England)
'For a man who was not remarkable for speed…John Reynolds was one of the most successful half-backs that have ever played…a wilier being never kicked a ball. He was full of originality and was one of the most perfect judges of an opponents' intentions I have ever known'. *Sporting Mail*, 13 October 1906.

RICHARDSON, Kevin

Position: Midfield
Born: Newcastle-upon-Tyne, 4 December 1962
Career: Everton (apprentice June 1978, professional December 1980); Watford (£225,000, September 1986); Arsenal (£200,000, August 1987); Real Sociedad, Spain (£750,000, July 1990); ASTON VILLA (£450,00, August 1991); Coventry City (£300,000, February 1995); Southampton (£150,000, September 1997); Barnsley (£300,000, July 1998); Blackpool (loan January–February 1999)

England
Caps: 1, Won: 1, Lost: 0, Drawn: 0

Kevin Richardson was an excellent midfield general who, in the first years of his professional career with Everton, won an FA Cup medal in 1984, a European Cup-Winners' Cup medal in 1985 and, in the same year,

gave opposition teams major headaches. The crowning glory of his Villa career was his leadership in the 1994 League Cup Final, when he operated in Villa's 5-man midfield to ensure Big Ron's plan to snuff out Manchester United's attack was successful. United were favourites but were outsmarted by counterattacking football. Richardson said afterward that this was better than winning League Championship medals, claiming 'this has to be better because everybody had written us off... I don't think we were under as much pressure as Manchester United. They only had to turn up to win, didn't they?' (McColl p.145).

a League Championship medal. Inexplicably, given his major role in winning the Championship, Everton then transferred him to mid-table Watford, the manager Graham Taylor snapping him up. His stay there was brief as Arsenal, like Taylor, saw his ability and took him to Highbury for three years, in which time he won another League Championship medal. They then sold him on to Real Sociedad in Spain for a very healthy profit.

Richardson, at 27, was still in his prime. After only a year Ron Atkinson brought him back from Spain with Dalian Atkinson, and he proved very effective for Atkinson's Villa side. Atkinson made him captain and, playing in front of the centre-backs, his ability to press while making incisive passes to the front players

His excellent form earned him an England cap that season, playing against Greece in a friendly at Wembley on 17 May. At 31 he could not expect to start an England career, but it was a justified pinnacle for his career. After this peak, his career went into decline and he was transferred to Coventry nine months later, having earned the respect and goodwill of football supporters in all of the three clubs he won medals for.

SMART, Tommy

Position: Full-back
Born: Blackheath, 20 September 1896
Died: 10 June 1968
Career: Blackheath Town, Army Football (1915–18), Halesowen (July

1919) VILLA (Janaury 1920), Brierley Hill Alliance (May 1934). Retired in 1936

England

Caps: 5, Won: 1, Lost: 2, Drawn: 2, Goals: 0

Tommy Smart was famous for being half of the full-back death and glory partnership with Thomas Mort after World War One. Smart became established earlier, breaking into the first team soon after being signed in January 1920 and playing till May 1934, and was slightly more successful, winning more caps and a winners' medal in the FA Cup in 1920, only months after being signed. Despite his abilities, he was never a first choice at full-back for England, his five caps coming at random over eight years, though he was consistent for Villa and played 451 games. This made him not only one of the 300 club but also the seventh in the all-time appearance table.

Like Tommy Mort, there are few accounts of his career. While full-backs are rarely crowd pleasers, it is disappointing that players who are vital to the team rarely have a high profile. With Smart, we are told he used to shout a Hindu war cry 'Thik Hai' which he had picked up on war service in India, that his size created apprehension among opposition forwards, and that he used to turn up to training on a bicycle wearing a flat cap – hardly unique in the 1920s.

As with other crucial players, there is very little hard information on his career, particularly at England level. His first cap on 9 April 1921 when in his first full season with Villa was in a 3–0 defeat by Scotland, and it was not suprising he was dropped. But when recalled in March 1924 he was vastly more experienced and playing with Mort could have expected a long partnership. Instead, as discussed in Mort's entry, the partnership was never recreated and random caps in April 1924, October 1925 and then after a five year break a final cap in 20 November 1929 makes little sense. If the selectors argued the Death or Glory partnership had not worked in a 2–1 defeat by Wales, why a 1–1 draw in 1924 (England's goalie scored

an own goal), 0–0 draw in 1925 and finally a 6–0 win against Wales in 1929 did not work in Smart's favour is not easy to understand. In his last three games, the defence did not do badly.

The very fact he spent his whole Division One career with one club means there was little written about him. Yet once he retired the defence began to leak goals and they were badly missed. Why the Death and Glory combination of Smart and Mort was only tried once by England – in March 1924, Smart's second cap – is only known to the selection committee.

SMITH, Steve

Position: Outside-left
Born: Differing sources give Hazelslade, Halesowen, 7 January 1874, Abbots Langley, 14 January 1874, or Abbots Bromley, 14 January 1874
Died: Benson, Oxon, 19 May 1935
Career: Cannock & Rugeley Colliery; Cannock Town; Rugeley Ceal; Hednesford Town (September 1891); ASTON VILLA (August 1893); Portsmouth (May 1901); New Brompton (July 1906, then player-manager December 1906–May 1908).

England
Caps: 1, Won: 1, Lost: 0, Drawn: 0, Goals: 1

Stephen Smith was one of the first choices for the great Villa side of the 1890s, certainly the most successful Villa side ever. An accomplished crosser of the ball who could whip in a stunning shot and rise to the big occasions, he was a miner in the South Staffordshire coalfield before being signed by the legendary Fred Rinder. Rinder organised the famous Barwick Street meeting, which led to him becoming senior director and laying the plans for Villa Park. He was not content with making the club's fortunes, however, and he sought the best players and was never more hands on than signing Steve Smith.

Rinder personally travelled to Hednesford, went hundreds of feet down the mine and negotiated with Smith, who was a haulage machine operator at the coal face. When he came to the surface after finishing his 10-hour shift, Smith signed the contract in the engine house – and Rinder lost his way in the dark. Luckily Rinder did not lose the contract Smith had signed; when he started playing for the Villa his record was outstanding.

Smith shared the left-wing berth with Albert Woolley in the Championship-winning side of 1893–94 before becoming first-choice left-winger. He won League medals in 1896, 1897, 1899 and 1900 and FA Cup-winners' medals in 1895 and 1897. He made 194 senior appearances in total, scoring 42 goals and making many others. Given his obvious talent, it is a mystery why he was only capped once, against Scotland on the 6 April 1895. Competition for the left-wing slot was intense, and he was admittedly short of physical stature, being only 5ft 4in. He was powerfully built at 11st 6lb, and Douglas Lammy quotes a report that states: 'with great speed he also passes very accurately and is further a safe shot at goal'. It continues by saying that he 'played a blinder in his international but was never picked again' (Douglas Lammy *Internationalists: Who's Who*, 1990, p.229).

Villa News & Record 1, 1 September 1906
One of the most effective players on the left wing since the time of Hodgetts. A particularly close dribbler, with a fine turn of speed, he was only robbed of the ball with difficulty, and with anything approaching a chance would centre most accurately. Being on the small side, he often suffered from the lungeous opponent, and while with the Villa suffered more than his share of hard knocks. Quiet and unassuming, he could always be relied upon to do his utmost.

SOUTHGATE, Gareth

Position: Centre-half
Born: Watford, 3 September 1970
Career: Crystal Palace, (YTS January 1987, professional January 1989), ASTON VILLA (£2.5 million, July 1995), Middlesbrough (£6.5 million, July 2001. Manager June 2006 till after the club's relegation in 2009. Sacked 20 October 2009, then TV commentator/pundit till appointed FA director of Elite Football 31 January 2011.

England
Caps: 57, Won: 29, Lost: 9, Drawn: 19, Goals: 2

Gareth Southgate was an outstanding central defender who won 42 caps while a Villa player and 15 while with Middlesbrough. He overcame one of the most public disasters in English football history – missing a decisive penalty in the shoot out against

Germany in the Euro 96 semi-final – because of his excellent standard of performance, and because no fan could seriously blame him for England's exit. He later made fun of the incident, appearing in a TV advert for pizza wearing a paper bag covering his head.

Southgate came through the ranks at Crystal Palace, becoming captain and leading them to the First Division Championship in 1994. The club was relegated in 1995 after one season and Southgate moved to Villa. He had been playing in central midfield, but Villa converted him into a centre-back, initially alongside Paul McGrath but then with a succession of partners, notably Ugo Ehiogu. In his first season Villa lifted the 1996 League Cup and qualified for the UEFA Cup (now Europa cup). He was ever present in the 1999–2000 season, by which time he was a seasoned England performer, but could see no way Villa would progress under John Gregory. He put in a transfer request after Villa's failure in the 2000 FA Cup 'in order to achieve in his career' – a stunning comment on the Villa at the time.

Ugo Ehiogu also fell out with Gregory and he was transferred to Middlesbrough for a record fee. Villa tried to hang on to Southgate, but after an uneasy year in which Southgate still turned in excellent performances, he was allowed to go, to rejoin Ehiogu at Middlesbrough. He slotted in immediately, winning the club's Player of the Year award in his first year.

Six months after joining Villa and emerging as a solid performer at centre-back with an excellent reading of the game and efficient marking of opposing forwards, Southgate was selected by Terry Venables and brought on as sub against Portugal in December 1995. He rose to the challenge and was clearly an international class performer, taken to the Euro 96 finals as a first-choice defender. He peformed superbly but sadly is best remembered for missing the sudden penalty in the semi-final shoot out against Germany. However as Paul Ince, Darren Anderton and Steve McManaman declined the challenge, Southgate could not be blamed for missing the shot. England had not practised taking penalties. Southgate went to the 1998 World Cup and the 2000 European Championship, but he did not make the 2002 World Cup.

Gareth Southgate was a level headed, committed player of integrity and skill. He played 242 games for Villa, and his performance on the field and behaviour off it was a model to young players. It is only regrettable that the club could not provide the success he desired. When he was appointed by the FA, Trevor Brooking said 'he has a wealth of experience as a player. He also is a high calibre individual'. Right on both counts.

SPENCER, Howard

Position: Full-back
Born: Edgbaston, Birmingham, 23 August 1875
Died: Four Oaks, Sutton Coldfield, 14 January 1940
Career: Albert Road School,

Handsworth, Birmingham; Stamford FC (1890); Birchfield All Saints (August 1891); Birchfield Trinity (January 1892); ASTON VILLA (amateur April 1892, professional June 1894–November 1907, director July 1909–May 1936)

England

Caps: 6, Won: 4, Lost: 1, Drawn: 1

Howard Spencer is a club legend who appeared in 295 games for the Villa before hanging up his boots at the age of 32. He never played for another club. A bridge between the great team of the 1890s and the early years of the 20th century, he won four League Championship medals, in 1896, 1897, 1899, 1900; two FA Cup-winners' medals, skippering the Villa to victory in the Cup Final of 1905; and earned two benefits (testimonials) in 1900 and

1906. Immensely popular for his personal as well as footballing qualities, he was taken onto the board in 1909 and served for nearly 30 years, in the end serving for 42 years in various capacities.

Like many full-backs, there were few major incidents to recall, and the qualities which made him successful were those of stopping the opposition and distributing the ball to the midfield – unspectacular but vital. He was noted for fair play, and years later he was honoured for his contribution to what became known as Villa tradition – skilful, attractive football played in the best spirit of the game. It is surprising that he only gained six England caps and that his career was patchy at international level – two games in 1897, one in 1900, one in 1903 and two in 1905, the year of the Cup victory. He was sufficiently highly thought of to be made captain of the team in his game in 1903, and again in 1905, however. He was the first Villa player to captain the national side.

At a time when the selectors still preferred Old Corinthians or other amateurs to captain the team, choosing a professional as captain meant that the player was thought to embody the qualities of the Corinthian in terms of fair play and playing to entertain rather than to win, and Spencer therefore had these qualities. He was still a winner at heart, though, as his record for both club and country shows. The *Book of Football* has a section written by him on how to play as a full-back.

Villa News & Record 1, 1 September 1906

'During a long and brilliant career has been one of England's best and fairest backs. Came into prominence during a junior international at Leamington in 1894. Tackles superbly, kicks with precision, and places with judgement: usually at his best when his side is in difficulties. Captained the team during 1903–04, 1904–05 and 1905–06.'

All in the Day's Sport, R. Allen, 1946

'[Spencer was] the outstanding example of what Aston Villa tradition on the football field came to mean. I shall never forget that neat looking, scrupulously clean playing, solid, safe looking full-back, tackling crisply, confidently, side tapping the ball into place for the long low-raking perfectly placed clearance. It seemed that he retained his control over the ball even after it had left his foot to hover, apparently, in the air, and land right at the foot of the man for whom it was intended'.

SPINK, Nigel

Position: Goalkeeper
Born: Chelmsford, 8 August 1958
Career: West Ham United, on schoolboy forms; Chelmsford City; ASTON VILLA (£4,000, January

1977); West Bromwich Albion (free transfer, January 1996); Millwall (£50,000, September 1997); Birmingham City (goalkeeping coach, early 1999); Swindon Town (goalkeeping coach, late 1999); Northampton Town (goalkeeping coach, 2000); Forest Green Rovers (player-joint manager, 2000–01).

Nigel was employed part-time by Steve Bruce at Birmingham and part-time at Forest Green Rovers prior to becoming full-time at Birmingham, moving with Bruce to Wigan and then Sunderland. He is currently employed as Sunderland's goalkeeping coach.

England

Caps: 1, Won: 0, Lost: 0, Drawn 1

Nigel Spink was an exceptionally capable goalkeeper who will always

have a special place in Villa's history because of the extraordinary second game he played for the first team, which happened to be the European Cup Final of 1982. Today it would be inconceivable that the club would face the most important game in its history with a rookie goalie on the bench, but it is a fact that, at 23, Nigel had only played one game for the first team – on Boxing Day 1979 – and did not expect to play when the match started. Indeed, while Nigel knew that Jimmy Rimmer had damaged his neck in training he stated: 'Jimmy always had knocks and strains but he always came through and strapped himself up and played. In my naivety I thought "don't even think about it. He's going to play."' Rimmer did play – for seven minutes – after which he handed over the gloves to Spink, and as Graham McColl says, he 'had no time to suffer from pre-match worries. He produced a nerveless performance against Bayern' to keep a clean sheet and carry off the prize (Graham McColl, p.110).

Rimmer would stay at Villa Park until the summer of 1983–84 but Nigel Spink had established himself. For the World Club Cup in December 1982 Rimmer stayed in goal, but for the European Super Cup in Mach 1983 Nigel Spink was in gaol against Barcelona in the Nou Camp and for the return at Villa Park. Villa triumphed despite tough play from

Barca, and Nigel later recalled, 'The home leg against Barcelona was a night that probably equalled the European Cup for excitement. The Spaniards tried every trick in the book' (Graham McColl, p.118). After that Nigel was number-one goalie. Manager Saunders had gone, however,and Tony Barton was not his equal. Villa were knocked out of the European Cup in 1983–84 by a Juventus side including Platini, Paolo Rossi, Tardelli, and Boniek. Nigel conceded four goals, but it was no disgrace against a great side including the European Footballer of the Year, Michel Platini.

Nigel played for England on 19 June 1983 in a friendly in Australia, coming on as substitute for Peter Shilton in the second half, in a 1–1 draw. There was the major problem for Nigel at England level: Shilton was a legendary goalkeeper, playing his 53rd international and on his way to becoming the most capped player in English football history. Only with exceptional performances and luck could Nigel Spink hope to replace Shilton. Unfortunately, Villa were in decline, with Chair Doug Ellis selling players to pay off a large debt and the new manager Graham Turner not resisting the policy. Nigel later commented, 'I felt a little bit that the team that had won the European Cup was broken up a little bit too early. Graham Turner had his own ideas about the team, but I felt some of those players he let go still had more to offer the club' (Graham McColl, p.122). He was clearly correct. Some of the players brought in were good – including a 17-year-old Tony Daley – but the club had over a decade of ups and downs, and Nigel never replaced Shilton. He lived the roller coaster that is life at Aston Villa and never wavered, despite losing first place for a time to Les Sealey. He was eventually overtaken by Mark Bosnich as first choice in February 1993 but served Villa for 20 years with 461 total appearances, more than any other Villa 'keeper. He is a legend in his own right.

STARLING, Ronnie

Position: Inside-left
Born: Pelaw on Tyne, Gateshead, 11 October 1909
Died: Sheffield, 17 December 1991
Career: Newcastle United (trial, November 1923); Usworth Colliery (January 1924); Washington Colliery (September 1924); Hull City (amateur June 1925, professional August 1927); Newcastle United (£3,750, May 1930); Sheffield Wednesday (£3,250, June 1932); ASTON VILLA (£7,500, January 1937); Nottingham Forest (player-coach, July 1948–June 1950); Beighton FC (February–April 1951).
Starling also guested for Northampton Town (1939–40), Hereford United (1940), Nottingham Forest (1939–40

and 1941–42), Walsall (1939–42) and Sheffield Wednesday (1940–41) during World War Two.

England
Caps: 2, Won: 0, Lost: 2, Drawn: 0

A coalminer after leaving school, Ronnie Starling had never been an immediately outstanding talent and went down the pit after being rejected by Newcastle United. Hull picked him up from the Washington Colliery works team, and Newcastle had to pay handsomely for missing him as a youth player. His was not a stellar talent and claims that, at his peak, he was better than Arsenal maestro of his era, Alex James, cannot be taken seriously. He was a great strategist,

however, who could influence a game, and he captained Sheffield Wednesday to the Cup against West Brom. He scored only 31 goals in 193 games in a Wednesday club starting to struggle, and he was transferred to Villa in January 1937, aged 27, after winning only one cap while in Sheffield, in April 1933.

Starling's decision to leave Sheffield was odd. While Wednesday were in decline, Villa were even worse off. Wednesday and Villa were the lost clubs of the mid-1930s, as the table shows. They had shadowed Arsenal in 1933 but then fell away badly.

Year (19)	33	34	35	36	37	38	39
Arsenal		1	1	1	6	3	1	5
Villa		2	13	13	21^R	9^{D2}	1^{D2}	12
Wednesday	3	11	3	20	22^R	17^{D2}	3^{D2}

^{R} = relegated
^{D2} = Division Two

When Starling was transferred, Villa had been relegated and were regrouping. Wednesday were falling apart. Villa with Starling got back in two seasons. Wednesday were still in Division Two when the war started so it can be said that Starling had made the right choice in going to Villa.

It was surprising he got a second cap, though. He had already won one cap while with Wednesday, and the selectors were giving a cap to a player who was in a successful team. By the time he got his second cap, however, it was April 1937 and Villa were stuck in Division Two. There is little logic in the decision, and this perhaps underlines the unprofessionalism of the selection committee at the FA more than anything else. It was certainly not an inspired decision – Scotland won the 1937 game as they had won the 1933 game and Starling was never capped again. All that one can really say about the selection is that by looking at the Villa in Division Two, the selectors may have noticed Frank Broome, who was to have a much better career in the national side.

TATE, Joseph Thomas

Position: Wing-half
Born: Old Hill, 4 August 1904
Died: Cradley Heath, 18 May 1973
Career: Birch Coppice Primitives; Grainger's Lane Primitives; Round Oak Steel Works; Brierley Hill; Cradley Heath (April 1923); ASTON VILLA, (£400, April 1925); Brierley Hill Alliance, player-manager (May 1935). Tate retired in May 1937 after breaking his right leg playing against Moor Green and went on to coach at the University of Birmingham (September 1937–45).

England

Caps: 3, Won: 1, Lost: 1, Drawn: 1

Along with the Scottish international Jimmy Gibson and Alec Talbot, Joe

Tate was one of the great half-back trio of the late 1920s and early 1930s known as 'Wind, Sleet and Rain'. All three men were over 6ft tall, and Peter Morris sees them as an ideal combination: Gibson the constructive artist on the right, Talbot a stopper centre-half, and Tate the ideal link between defence and attack (Peter Morris, p.133). Like other players in the inter-war years, Tate was an excellent club player who was initially seen as a squad player rather than a major talent, as his fee of £400 when signed in April 1925 indicated. He was bought to understudy Frank

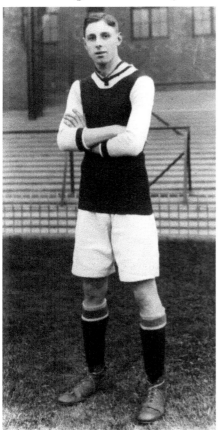

Moss and was overshadowed by him until Moss was transferred in January 1929. He did have potential, which earned him a trial for England in 1925 (Whites against Colours), but he did not impress until he gained regular experience as Moss faded. He was then a stalwart of the Villa squad until injuries brought his career to an end.

His performances in the 1930–31 season, when Villa chased Arsenal for the title, convinced the selectors that he should be tried at international level. In spring 1931 he gained two caps in two friendlies abroad, against France and Belgium. Eric Houghton and Pongo Waring were in the same team, making a rare Villa threesome in both matches, and he won a third cap in the home internationals against Wales in 1932 alongside George Brown. Having reached the peak aged 28, however, he was affected by injuries, one of which is said to have nearly broken his neck, and he was not capped again (Peter Morris, p.133).

Once he had overtaken Moss in the pecking order, Tate was a regular for five years, making 193 senior appearances for the Villa. His last few years were marked by frequent absences and he only played one game for the first team in his last two years. His career ended in 1935 having never really hit the heights, and he remains a somewhat shadowy figure.

THOMPSON, Thomas

Position: Inside-forward
Born: Fencehouses, near Houghton-le-Spring, County Durham, 10 December 1929
Career: Lumley YMCA (1944); Newcastle United (August 1946); ASTON VILLA (£12,000, September 1950); Preston North End (£28,500, June 1955); Stoke City (£10,000, July 1961); Barrow (£5,000, March 1963–May 1965)
Thompson retired and returned to Preston as a carpenter.

England
Caps: 2, Won: 1, Lost: 0, Drawn: 1

Thompson was a talented player who made a good career in the game without breaking though at the very top. He was signed by the Villa in 1950 as a player with real potential, but after he failed to establish himself in the England team following his first cap on 20 October 1951 his development stalled. The Villa management, struggling with a club in decline, could not improve his skills or achieve success for the team, something which came to be a bone of contention. Neither of Villa's most talented players in the early 1950s could tolerate the decline of the club, and after Villa were defeated by Doncaster Rovers of the Second Division Danny Blanchflower demanded a transfer and got it. Thompson then followed suit and the club transferred him to Preston, replacing him with the established England international Jackie Sewell. Sewell was no more, and no less, successful than Thompson had been as the set up at Villa Park was no longer competitive at the highest level, but that is another story. The key issue was that after nearly five years at Villa Park, Thompson could not see himself being successful with the Villa.

Thompson was certainly not a failure at Villa Park; it was the club that failed. A squad which included Colin Gibson, Johnny Dixon, Trevor Ford and Les Smith promised but failed to deliver. As Thompson was only 20 when he arrived at Villa Park, he could have been polished into a diamond. Sadly, his talent was not developed. At Preston he worked well with the legendary Tom Finney, well enough to gain a second cap, but without ever hitting the heights. At Stoke he played with another legend, Stanley Matthews, then in the Indian summer of his superb career.

Thompson also represented England B and the Football League side as well as winning his two full caps. He scored 76 goals in 165 games for Villa, an excellent return, and overall scored 224 goals in 450 League games. His best return, however, was at Preston, where he scored 117 goals in 188 games alongside Finney, a far better player than any at the Villa in his time bar Blanchflower. A very good player, Tommy Thompson can be considered not quite good enough for the very top of the game. Had he not played for a declining Villa in an era when its coaching skills were limited, would he have gained more success?

VASSELL, DARIUS

Position: Striker
Born: Birmingham 13 June 1980
Career: Birmingham and District Schools; ASTON VILLA (YTS June 1996, professional April 1998); Manchester City (£2 million, July 2005); Ankaragucu, Turkey (free transfer, July 2009); Leicester City (free transfer, October 2010)

England
Caps: 22, Won: 8, Lost: 5, Drawn: 9, Goals: 6

Darius Vassell was brought up on the Birmingham–Sutton Coldfield border, going to school in Erdington and Wylde Green. He came through the schoolboy system and was taken on by the Villa School of Excellence. He set a then club record by scoring 39 goals for the youth team in a single season. He made his first-team debut as substitute in a 3–1 win against Middlesbrough in August 1998. He took two seasons to establish himself in the side and then became a regular in the 2000–01 season, but while he played 28 games he only scored five goals.

His prime period was from the 2001–02 season to the 2003–04 season. In these three seasons he made 121 appearances and scored 35 goals – a goal rate of 29 per cent, or nearly one every three games, a good record. However, his form dropped off in the 2004–05 season. He played only 22 games in total for the Villa scoring only three goals – a 13.6 per cent goal rate, or little more than a goal every seven games.

At the end of the season he was transferred to Manchester City for £2 million. There he had a moderately successful record over the next three season of 110 appearances, scoring 21 goals or 19 per cent – one goal every five matches. After playing only two games in 2008–09 under manager Sven-Goran Eriksson, he moved to Turkish side Ankaragucu for 2009–10. Alas, the club had financial problems, and he returned home to rejoin Eriksson at Championship side Leicester City in October 2010.

The 2001–02 season, his first really successful season, saw him called up by England on 13 February 2002, when he made one of the most spectacular entrances ever, scoring England's only goal with a bicycle kick which flew past the stunned Dutch goalkeeper. In one of the best soccer photos of all time, Edwin van der Saar has a look of panic on his face like the famous Edvard Munch painting *The Scream*.

Vasseell set himself an impossibly high standard with that first goal, and he never quite fulfilled his initial promise. He tended to be used as an impact player, being substituted four times in his first six games, while for the final 16 appearances he was used as a super sub to reinforce the attack against tiring defences. Overall, he was subbed for Michael Owen seven times in his England career and Wayne Rooney, the rising star at the time, three times. Both his last substitutions were to replace Rooney. His record of six goals in 22 games, two of which came in a friendly against Iceland, was disappointing.

The final chapter in his England career came when he missed the final penalty in the quarter-finals of Euro 2004 on 24 June 2004 after coming on as sub for injured Wayne Rooney. The miss put England out of the competition. Vassell never appeared for England again. At his best, Darius Vassell was a strong, pacy forward who caused defences serious problems. While he was not an abundant scorer, he is remembered for some fine individual goals.

VAUGHTON, Oliver Howard

Position: Inside-left
Born: Aston, Birmingham, 2 January 1861
Died: Birmingham, January 1937
Career: Waterloo FC; Birmingham FC

(no relation to current Birmingham City); Wednesbury Strollers; ASTON VILLA (August 1880, retired June 1888 due to serious thigh injury).

Worked for the family silversmith's business in the Jewellery quarter which made the replacement FA Cup for the original Cup stolen in 1895 after Villa won it. Vice President of Villa 1923, director September 1924–December 1932, then life member of the club, February 1933.

England

Caps: 5, Won: 2, Lost: 3, Drawn: 0, Goals: 6

In Villa's first golden decade of the 1880s, after winning the club's first trophy, the Birmingham Cup in 1880, Vaughton was a key member of the squad which made the transition from a local club recruiting part-time players to a full time outfit taking the game professionally – though he himself always remained an amateur. A most effective inside-left, he scored at a rate of a goal every two games until a thigh injury forced him out in the 1887–88 season and eight years in the team. He scored 15 goals in 30 FA Cup appearances. These were the only official games: no one knows how many friendlies he played in.

Vaughton remained amateur and was the only non professional in the team which won the FA Cup for the first time in 1887. He had already played five games for England, playing alongside Arthur Brown as joint first Villa caps. He played three games in domestic friendlies against the Home countries in 1882, and two in the Home Championship in 1884. Though he was never recalled, he had made a permanent mark in the record books by being the first player in the history of world football to score five goals in an international match – the 13–0 victory against the Irish on 18 February 1882.

Vaughton was enormously popular playing alongside Archie Hunter and the squad which became a national force in the 1880s. He was regarded as playing the game in the right sporting spirit, playing for satisfaction and not money. He was a competent skater, winning the England Ice skating Championship, played cricket for Warwickshire and Staffordshire, was a County hockey player, a racing cyclist and a first-class swimmer. As professionalism became established there was less and less place for players who spread themselves so thinly, and Vaughton was one of the last of the dying breed of the amateur playing for fun.

Note: *Aston Villa: The Complete Record* (2010) says he began his own jewellery business after retiring in 1888. But he had always worked in the family firm, which dated back to 1819, which is why he was an amateur. The building in Livery Street still exists, and the company name is still used but by another company in the jewellery quarter.

Villa News & Record 1, 1 September 1906
The people's favourite, and one of Archie Hunter's pet pupils. He dribbled like angel and shot like a demon. Whatever he did, he did well, and was neatness personified. Could scarcely be played in the wrong position, and was saturated through and through with the Aston Villa spirit. Made a famous wing in company with Eli Davies.

WALKER, Billy

Position: Forward
Born: Wednesbury, 29 October 1897
Died: Sheffield, 28 November 1964
Career: Walsall Boys; Hednesford Town; Wednesbury Old Athletic; Wednesbury Old Park; Darlaston; ASTON VILLA (amateur December 1914, professional June 1920–November 1933); Sheffield Wednesday, (manager, December 1933–November 1937); Chelmsford City (manager, January 1938–October 1938); Nottingham Forest (manager, March 1939–July 1960). Walker played eight games for Forest during World War Two.

See Pantheon section for full details.

WALLACE, Charles William

Position: Outside-right
Born: Southwick, near Sunderland, 20 January 1885
Died: 7 January 1970
Career: Sunderland and District Schools; Southwick FC (1903); Crystal Palace (July 1905); ASTON VILLA (£500, May 1907); Oldham Athletic (£1,000, May 1921)

Wallace retired in 1923 to become a painter and decorator, working at Villa Park part time in the boot room with the kit, as a steward and mentor to Aston Villa's Junior Ordnance

Corps team in the late 1930s, leading them to the runners'-up spot behind West Bromwich Albion in their League in 1938–39. He continued to work for the Villa as an odd-job man after World War Two.

England

Caps: 3, Won: 2, Lost: 1, Drawn: 0

When Charles Wallace signed in May 1907 aged 22, the fee broke the Villa transfer record and he became a vital part of the League Championship side of 1910 and the FA Cup sides of 1913 and 1920. After five years the *Villa News* on 26 October 1912 praised him as a team player saying, 'He never hesitates to fetch the ball himself, and in this respect is a much more valuable player than the man who…is purely content to wait for the ball to be put to him before he shows his mettle'.

He was highly valued as a team member and played 349 games for Villa, scoring 57 goals. He was the first player to miss a penalty in an FA Cup Final, in 1913, but took the corner which lead to the winning goal. That he gained only three full caps shows he was possibly not the most talented player in his position at that time, but remarkably he won them over a long period before and after World War One: one in 1913, when he could have won more, another in 1914, and then his final

cap in 1920, aged 35. The selectors, perhaps unsure of the best talent after the long break, clearly saw him as a proven player despite his age, noting him as a man who was still playing for Villa in the First Division and was about to win an FA Cup place – a good bet for the team in an uncertain period. His final cap against Scotland was put down to his display in the Cup semi-final against Chelsea. The selectors had praised three other players, one of whom was Barson, yet none of them was picked. Selection policy is obscure.

In addition to his caps this speedy winger represented the Football League five times and played in three trials.

Villa News & Record, 23 April 1913, p.548
'Few players can change the direction of their run with the same adroitness. While at the top of speed for a sprint along the touchline, Wallace will suddenly swerve towards the middle of the field with a facility that leaves defenders wondering what has become of him. He centres with almost uncanny exactitude, placing the ball high to the far side of the goalmouth or passing along the ground to a colleague who is not covered by opponents. He puts tremendous power behind his shots, which are exceptionally accurate for an extreme wing player.'

7 April 1920 p.4
'The team is identical with that selected to represent the Football League…[but] Wallace gets the place at outside right. The Villa man was seen at his very best in the semi-final against Chelsea. He was selected to play against Scotland in 1913 but was unable to accept due to the sudden death of his father.'

WARING, Thomas 'Pongo'

Position: Centre-forward
Born: Birkenhead 12 October 1906. Died, 20 December 1980
Career: Tranmere Celtic (1922); Tranmere Rovers (professional February 1926); ASTON VILLA (£4,700 February 1928); Wolverhampton Wanderers (July 1936); Tranmere Rovers (October 1936); Accrington Stanley (November 1936 to July 1939); Bath City (August–September 1939)
Waring worked as a docker after the war, playing for local teams.

England

Caps: 5, Won: 4, Lost: 1, Drawn: 0

Pongo Waring, the nickname coming from a cartoon character, ranked with Billy Walker and Eric Houghton as a great Villa forward of the 1930s, to a considerable extent overshadowing Frank Broome who continued the tradition of great Villa forwards without gaining the recognition he deserved. Pongo Waring was a mythical figure with many stories but not a lot of information on how he played. He was clearly a big, strong centre-forward of a type beloved by the Villa crowd through history, writing his own record book in the scoring records he and the team set. Not for nothing does Peter Morris point out that he was the centre of the most prolific Villa scoring machine in history. He himself scored 167 goals in 225 games for Villa – an astonishing average of one every 100 minutes of play over an eight-year career.

The player remains elusive, however, despite the many tales about him. One of the more reliable commentators, Billy Walker, who wrote about Waring in his autobiography, adds to the mystery by reporting that he hardly ever trained and was under-prepared – posing the question how he achieved the goal record he did.

Pongo Waring was undoubtedly a larger-than-life character and lived on in the memories and gossip handed down through supporters talk for many years. It is a sign of how popular he was among supporters that on two occasions fans contributed poetry about him to the *News and Record*, first in September 1930 and then in February 1931, during the famous goal glut season when the team scored a

record total of 128 League goals. Pongo scored four goals at least twice, firstly in the opening game of the season in a 3–4 victory over Manchester United at Old Trafford, and then again in a home victory 4–2 over Sunderland on 18 February, and was the highest scorer with 49 goals – still an individual record. The survey from the International Federation of Football History and Statistics (IHFS) comments that Waring was: 'Extremely self assured with a colourful character. The central figure of many endless stories.' p.119. Unfortunately the stories do not add up to a full picture. Pongo is the only Villa player to have had a racehorse named after him – by Villa supporter John Peutherer.

POEMS TO TOM WARING
Villa News & Record

September 27/29 1930, p.72
Here, a live wire, is gay Tom Waring,
The idol of the crowd:
He goes for goal in robust manner,
And we are mighty proud.
On form he's one that takes some watching,
And 'off-days' are not yet;
And thirteen goals he's scored already,
And more he's sure to get...
FER

21 February 1931, p.374
The studious football fanatic

Regrets he did not see the trick
Of all four goals that Waring shot
When Sunderland came to our plot
I'm glad I went, despite the ground
Was moved about as men turned round
And shoved a piece of Warwickshire
From here to there, and there to here;
Because we saw the old traditions
Gaily upheld by new additions....

Peter Morris on Pongo Waring:
'Tom "Pongo" Waring, Aston Villa's finest centre-forward since Harry Hampton, arrived on the scene in February 1928 and galvanised the club's forwards into the most prolific scoring unit in Villa's history. During Waring's peak years as leader of the attack (1928–33) the Villa forwards enjoyed a continuous goal glut which reached its climax in 1930–31 when they scored 128 goals in 42 matches, a First Division record which still stands. Although Waring scored less than half of these – Walker, Beresford, and Eric Houghton also reached double figures – the centre-forward himself netted 49, to establish a new individual record for the club.' p.134

Billy Walker on Pongo Waring
'He was one of the most likeable of lads, but he clowned his way through life. Big hearted, too, he would give his last shilling to a down and out and go without himself...There were no rules for Pongo. Nobody knew when

he would turn up for training...Sometimes I would persuade him to come on the ground with me to practice a move, but after ten minutes he would kick the ball into the stand and say "I've had enough", and that was that...I never tried to bully Pongo Waring because I knew that if I ever did he would pack up. But by giving him a bit of chaff there was no length to which we couldn't get him to go for us'.

Soccer in the Blood p.27

WARNOCK, Stephen

Position: Left-back
Born: Ormskirk, Lancashire, 12 December 1981
Career: Rufford Colts; Liverpool Academy; England Youth (first cap aged 16); Bradford City (loan 2002); Coventry City (loan 2003–04); Liverpool (1998–2007); Blackburn Rovers (2007–09); ASTON VILLA (2009–present)

England

Caps: 2, Won: 1, Lost: 1, Drawn: 0, Goals: 0

Stephen Warnock was a product of the Liverpool academy, making his Liverpool debut in 2004 in the first leg of a UEFA Champion's League match. Warnock impressed in his first season 2004–05, but mainly as a left-winger who challenged the experienced Harry Kewell for a first-

team slot. In his second season 2005–06 he was converted to left-back, rotating with John Arne Riise. He made 67 appearances before being transferred to Blackburn Rovers on 22 January 2007 for an undisclosed fee. He was a talented and hard-working player who impressed the fans, winning fans' Player of the Season when on loan at Coventry, and 2008–09 Player of the Season award with Blackburn Rovers.

Although he had played relatively few games for Liverpool, he was called into the England squad for the first time on 29 August 2005 due to the lack of quality left-backs. However it was not till he was at Blackburn Rovers that Fabio Capello called him into the squad again in May 2008 for the friendlies against the USA and Trinidad and Tobago. He made his first appearance for England against the latter on 1 June 2008, coming on as substitute for Wayne Bridge in the 84th minute. This gave him one of the shortest England careers on record.

With Ashley Cole established as one of the best full-backs in the world and Bridge a good second, his England career appeared limited. When Bridge retired from international football as part of a row involving John Terry's relationship with his then girlfriend, the way was open for Warnock to look to resurrect his England career.

By 2009, with the World Cup looming, Warnock was transferred to Villa. Wilfred Bouma, Villa's first-choice at left-back, had suffered an horrific injury which eventually ended his career. Cover for Bouma had already been provided by Nicky Shorey, but this did not work out, and Warnock was signed on a four-year contract by Martin O'Neill on 27 August 2009 and given the number-25 shirt. When Bouma retired,

Warnock got his number-three shirt. Warnock's impressive play in the early part of 2009–10 earned him a recall to the England squad. However, his way was still blocked by Cole, and he did not play. He was, however, named in the 30-man and 22-man squads for the World Cup in South Africa and travelled to the tournament with every chance of an appearance. It did not happen. Cole still blocked his way.

It was not until 17 November 2010 that he was called into action for the last 20 minutes of a friendly against France, giving him an England career of less than half an hour. The record of two games over two years apart shows he was not able to dislodge the players in front of him in the rankings. His first match 1 June 2008, was a 3–0 Victory over Trinidad and Tobago, Second match 17 November 2010, a 1–2 defeat by France.

Good form for the Villa in the 2009–10 season, when he played 41 games, did not continue into his second season. He played most games in the first half of the season, but from 13 September to 28 December he picked up eight yellow cards and, after a poor performance in the 4–0 defeat by Man City, lost his place. He has shown himself to be a very good full-back at his best, but only by playing at his best continually will he achieve with the Villa.

WHATELEY, Oliver 'Olly'

Position: Inside-forward
Born: Coventry, 8 August 1861
Died: Birmingham, October 1926
Career: Gladstone Unity; Coventry (1878); ASTON VILLA (July 1880)
Whateley retired with facial cancer in May 1888 and never played soccer seriously again, moving to London to pursue his career as a commercial artist.

England

Caps: 2, Won: 1, Lost: 1, Drawn: 0, Goals 2

An amateur like Howard Vaughton, Oliver Whateley has left far less of a record behind him than Vaughton did. Whateley is said to have been an aggressive inside-forward with a fierce shot, who scored nine goals in 19 FA Cup appearances, but his overall record in the years before the formation of the League, when he retired, is obscure. An artist and designer by profession, he was the son of the Birmingham councillor, James Whateley, and was, like Vaughton, one of the middle-class amateurs involved in Villa in the years before professionalism made football a full-time occupation. He may have played in the Cup Victory of 1887, but even this is obscure. He was good enough to be picked for England twice, scored twice in a 7–0 win against Ireland, and played a second match against the Scots, both in 1883, but sadly he has left very little information behind him beyond his reputation as fierce shot – he was famous for shooting along the ground in what became known as his 'daisy cutter'. He kept in touch with the club, and a letter from Whateley is in the *Villa News* for 19 September 1908.

Villa News & Record, 1 September 1906
'As a deadly shot and goal-getter, he achieved quite a remarkable distinction, and probably scored more dazzling goals than any other player of his period. Slipping through opponents by his smart dribbling and clever feinting, he won positions for himself with astonishing celerity. One of the diminishing "band of brothers" who helped build up Aston Villa's early fame, and still kindly remembered.'

18 November 1909
'Goalkeepers of that generation will still tell you…he would send in shots at difficult angles with amazing speed and certainty, and it was a striking feature of them that they hardly ever left "the carpet". Beyond that they often swerved so much that they fairly flabbergasted the finest 'keepers…It was an actual fact that he could put "side" on a ball like a billiard player…but, of course, not to such an extent.'

WHELDON, George Frederick 'Fred'

Position: Inside-left
Born: Langley Green, Oldbury, 1 November 1869
Died: St George's, Worcester, 13 January 1924
Career: School teams; West Bromwich Albion (trial October–November 1888); Small Heath (February 1890); ASTON VILLA (£350, June 1896); West Bromwich Albion (£100, August 1900); Queen's Park Rangers (£400, December 1901); Portsmouth (£150, August 1902); Worcester City (July 1904–May 1906) Wheldon also played county cricket for Worcestershire and Camarthenshire and later became a publican in Worcester.

England
Caps: 4, Won: 4, Lost: 0, Drawn: 0, Goals: 6

Fred Wheldon had the reputation of being a brilliant footballer who never gained the national recognition he deserved. While selection is always clouded by the issue of who at the time was a better player in that position, Wheldon's record does suggest a late developer who

achieved very high standards, with the *News & Record* arguing that he was, at his best, 'the finest inside-left England possessed'. A Villa view is likely to be biased, but it is backed up by the independent view of two contemporary writers who praised Wheldon's combination with other players.

Wheldon started at Small Heath (now Birmingham City) and scored 84 goals in 134 games. He helped Small Heath top the Second Division in its first year of operation in 1893, when promotion was not allowed, and again in 1984 when the promotion system began operating. Blues struggled in Division One, however, and were relegated in 1896, at which time Villa had won the second of their League titles. Wheldon jumped ship for the bigger club, won League

Championship medals in 1897, 1898, and 1900, and the 1897 FA Cup when Villa did the double. He averaged a goal a game over 267 first-class outings, totalling 156 for the two Birmingham clubs. He was also the first player to play for the three local clubs, though his form understandably declined at West Brom, aged over 31.

He was regarded as an excellent team man as well as goalscorer, and given his record it is hard to see why he only gained four caps and four inter-League games. As England won all four of the games in which he played, and he scored six goals to give him an excellent scoring rate of 1.5 per game, he certainly did not let the side down. The others picked for his position must have been tremendous players.

Villa News & Record 1, 1 September 1906

'At one period of his long and brilliant career, Fred Wheldon's services would have been accepted by any club in the country. When at his best, he was undoubtedly the best inside-forward England possessed. His command of the ball, his adaptability to prevailing conditions, combined with his dodging, his swerving and his deadly shooting, made him a great player in the highest company.'

Sports Argus, 6 April 1901

'No man ever helped the half-back

behind him better than Fred Wheldon did. He always fell back when he was wanted…a born tackler.'

Gibson and Pickford, *Association Football*, 1906, Vol 2, p.43, on Wheldon's combination with Fred Spiksley and Ernest Needham in the 3–1 victory against the Scots in 1898: 'The three men filled into one another's methods like hands into their proper gloves, and all the brilliance of the Scots defence was dumbfounded and beaten'. (Wheldon scored the opening goal from an assist by Charlie Athersmith.)

WILKES, Albert

Position: Wing-half (defender)
Born: West Bromwich, October 1875
Died: Bromsgrove, 9 December 1936
Career: Oldbury Town; Walsall (1896); ASTON VILLA (May 1898); Fulham (June 1907); Chesterfield (February – May 1909)

Wikes had a photography business in West Bromwich, but retired when fire badly damaged it. It was rebuilt and flourished with a sporting angle, becoming one of the most important early photo libraries in the Edwardian era. His son took it over until the whole collection was sold to the London-based company Colorsport. Wilkes took up refereeing and was appointed to the board at Villa Park in September 1934.

England
Caps: 5, Won: 2, Lost: 0, Drawn: 3, Goals: 1

Albert Wilkes is another of those players who have left virtually no record behind, though he held down a place in a highly successful Villa side and must have been more than just a good player at wing-half – the position in the old WW formation alongside a single centre-half to double up as defenders and suppliers of the five man attack. Comments like 'scrupulously fair' and 'straight as a die' do not explain how the man held down his position in a Villa side with an exceptional record.

Wilkes was signed from Walsall just in time for the Championship-winning side of 1899. He won five England caps in a side that remained unbeaten and gained two League

Championship medals, though whether he was in the 1905 FA Cup-winning side is obscure. His reputation lasted and he became a director of the club. Thirty Villa players attended his funeral in 1936. Given this excellent record, why the record books need to be padded out with information on his photography, singing, and swimming heroics, is hard to understand. He had to be a fine player – but he is lost in obscurity.

6 1, 1 September 1906
'Scrupulously fair and honest in tackling, a willing worker and an adept at finding openings for goal in big games. A quiet, unostentatious player of the untiring order, he has done his share of raising the tone of football on and off the field. "Straight as a die", he is a general and deserved favourite.'

WITHE, Peter

Position: Centre-forward
Born: Liverpool, 30 August 1951
Career: Skelmersdale (amateur 1968–69); Smith Coggins FC (1969–70); Southport (amateur July 1970, professional August 1971); Preston North End (briefly mid-1971); Barrow (trialist December 1971); Port Elizabeth (South Africa) 1972–73; Wolverhampton Wanderers (£13,500, October 1973); Portland Timbers, USA (May 1975); Birmingham City (£50,000, August 1975); Nottingham

Forest (£42,000, September 1976); Newcastle United (£200,000, August 1978); ASTON VILLA (£500,000, May 1980); Sheffield United (free transfer July 1985); Birmingham City (1987); Huddersfield Town (player-coach July 1988); ASTON VILLA (assistant manager/coach to Doctor Jo Venglos, January–October 1991), Wimbledon (manager October 1991–January 1992); Port Vale (Football in the Community officer 1992–95), ASTON VILLA (chief scout 1998); Thailand (national team coach/soccer advisor 2000–01); Indonesia (national team coach 2004–07)
Now lives in Australia.

England
Caps: 11, Won: 5, Lost: 3, Drawn: 3, Goals: 1
Choosing the great club players is never easy. Great achievement for the club, outstanding work ethic, national recognition all have to be part of it. But there has to be an X factor which makes a player memorable. For Peter Withe, this is easy to see. The moment in Rotterdam when he scored the winning goal in the European Cup Final will never be forgotten. But he deserves to be remembered for far more than one goal. Often regarded as a journeyman who relied on strength rather than skill, his technical abilities were overlooked till he arrived at Villa under Ron Saunders.

He was signed to fill a gap in the

centre of the attack after Andy Gray left for an England record fee of £1,469,00. The fee for Withe of £500,000 suggested Villa were getting a third of the player they had lost. Nothing could have been further from the truth. Although Withe had won a Championship medal with Brian Clough's Nottingham Forest in 1978, he had never achieved his full potential. Villa's Championship season, with the coaching of Saunders, Tony Barton and Roy McClaren, made Peter Withe into an international player.

He had always had more skill commentators credited him with – Gordon Cowans, definitely a flair player, later said that 'Every time someone on our side had the ball, Peter was always available to be hit. He'd pull off to make angles or he'd pull away from the shoulders of people... He had a lot more ability than people gave him credit for. He had good control, could hold the ball up and knock balls down for people. He scored a lot of goals with his head as well'. (McColl p.99).

He was the player Brian Clough missed. Anxious to raise the money to make the flair player Trevor Francis the first million-pound transfer, he sold Withe to Newcastle in the old Second Division for £200,000. Saunders spotted that this was a waste of talent, signed him as the final piece in the jigsaw for his third Villa team,

and hit the jackpot.

The essence of a Saunders side was blending flair, solid hard work and a team ethic where each player worked for the good of the whole. Withe fitted in perfectly. In the 1981 attack, Morley and Shaw had bucket loads of flair. But neither would have been as good without Withe. He finished his first season at Villa with a second Championship medal with wide recognition that his contribution was more than just the goals scored – though he topped the scoring charts with 20 goals from 36 games, jointly with Spur's Steve Archibald. His real value was that he tied up the opposition defenders. Lurking on the edge of the box, Withe stopped the opposition moving out to cut off Morley and Shaw. His ability to hold the ball up while the attack developed made him a nightmare to mark. He had an almost telepathic understanding with young Gary Shaw, and the combination of strength, fitness and tactical awareness made him a formidable centre-forward.

The following May he reached the high point of his personal career, scoring the winning goal in the European Cup Final in Rotterdam. Villa should have built on this success, but Ron Saunders had resigned and his successor Tony Barton struggled to cope with Doug Ellis demanding he cut the club's

financial deficit. Despite some success, notably winning the European super Cup against Barcelona, and losing to a great Juventus side in the 1982–83 European Cup, Villa were on the slide and Withe did not score in these later European matches. However his contribution to the European and Super Cup victories were immense. Alas the impetus Saunders had provided faded after that. Barton left with increasing financial problems facing the club. In the summer of 1985 Withe took a free transfer to Sheffield Wednesday as new manager

Graham Turner tried to rebuild the side while cutting costs. Withe later said it was 'the biggest wrench of my career'. He appeared 233 times for Villa, scoring 92 goals – an excellent ratio of a goal every 2.53 games.

England Career

He played 11 games for England over five years, all while at the Villa. He played three games in the 1980–81 season, all after Villa had won the League, and three in 1982, but despite being in the frame England Manager Ron Greenwood did not play him in the 1982 World Cup. Wikipedia say Withe 'Was the first ever English player representing Aston Villa to feature in a World Cup finals squad' (in Espana '82), but this is misleading. He was taken, but did not play. The first Villa player to play in a World Cup Final was Steve Hodge in 1986.

The problem was that he was in competition with Paul Mariner of Ipswich for the centre-forward job, and Mariner was a more regular goalscorer. In his 11 games for England, Withe only scored one goal. This was in his third season as an England striker, 1982–83, in his seventh match, in a game against the Hungarians. He played two more that season, one in the autumn of 1983, then over a year later in November 1984, in an 8–0 romp against the Turks. But he was not one of the scorers, and his England career was over.

Peter Withe will always be celebrated for the two title-winning sides he played in, and it is perhaps significant that they were both for unfashionable provincial clubs. He was a skilled, brave and hard working player, loved by fans who valued old fashioned centre-forward play. This was perhaps not what the modern game needed at international level, and his international record was not as one of the great goalscorers. But there was never any doubt about his contribution and commitment in every game he played, and the respect he gained from all quarters. He has never been forgotten and was called in to be assistant manager during the managership of Dr Jo Venglos.

YORK, Richard

Position: Outside-right
Born: Handsworth, Birmingham, 25 April 1899,
Died, Handsworth, Birmingham, 9 December 1969
Career: Icknield St Council School, Hockley; King Edward Grammar School, Aston; Birmingham Boys (captain); Handsworth Royal; Birchfield Rangers; RAF (commissioned); Chelsea (guest); ASTON VILLA (professional 1919); Port Vale (June 1931); Brierley Hill Alliance (August 1932–May 1934); ASTON VILLA (third team and also coach 1948–49)

York also guested for Chelsea during World War One.

England

Caps: 2, Won: 0, Lost: 2, Drawn: 0, Goals: 0

Richard York was one of the brightest stars from the era before and after the first world war when Villa could still look into the inner city areas around Aston and find outstanding talent. York went to elementary school in Hockley, not two miles from the ground, in a building still standing almost underneath the Hockley fly over on the Soho road. From an early age he showed outstanding sprinting ability. He was training with the Birchfield Harriers as a sprinter from the age of eight. However he was also an outstanding school boy footballer, following a similar course to Billy Walker over in the Black Country, though a school year behind Walker. Unlike Walker, his academic talent led him to a Grammar School education, but like Walker he was not deflected from a football career.

York was in fact one of a select few who have represented England at school boy and full international level. This might have come to nothing, not merely because of the high failure rate among schoolboy internationals, but because in World War One he was commissioned as a fighter pilot, a particularly dangerous

occupation. However, he survived, returned to Aston and made the first of his 390 senior games for Villa in the opening Saturday of the first season after the war, 1919–20. he was initially right-half but switched to replace Charlie Wallace on the right wing in the later part of the 1920–21 season. It was this move which made his career. He had not taken part in the successful 1920 FA Cup campaign, but from the start of the 1921–22 season he was first choice for nine seasons, ever present in 1926–1926 and 1928–1929 to become a member of the 300 club.

York was not a prolific goalscorer, scoring only 86 goals in nine seasons for a ratio of around a goal every four games, but was an excellent provider

for other forwards. Sadly, he did not establish himself in the England side, and though he was tried in two games against Scotland in April 1922 and April 1926 both were lost and he failed to break through permanently at international level. His second game, a defeat by Wales in 1926, was as part of a Villa trio in which Billy Walker gained his eighth cap and Mort his third. Mort and York never played for England again, unlike Walker who was recalled after one game out.

YOUNG, Ashley Simon

Position: Winger
Born: Stevenage, 9 July 1985
Career: Watford Youth team (2000–02); Watford professional (2002–07, 101 appearances, 20 goals); ASTON VILLA (18 January 2007–present, £8 million, rising to £9.75 million)

England: (Up to and including 9 February 2011)
Caps: 12, Won: 8, Lost: 2, Drawn: 2, Goals: 1

Ashley Young was born in Stevenage, attending the John Henry Newman School, where he played school football alongside Lewis Hamilton, later the World Formula 1 Driving Championship. He was initially turned down by the Watford Academy but accepted after working to improve his game. He made his first-team debut at age 18 in September 2003, scoring as substitute. He made five substitute appearances that season, breaking through in the 2004–05 season to make 34 League appearances in the Championship to win the Watford Young Player of the Season award. In the promotion-winning 2005–06 he made 41 League appearances as the club rose through the Play-offs to win promotion.

His form at Watford in the 2005–06 season earned him a call up to Peter Taylor's England Under-21 League squad to face an Italian Serie B squad, and he was called up to the full Under-21 squad in September 2006, playing the last 15 minutes. This earned him a place in the 2007 UEFA Under-21 Championship. His first season in the top flight, 2006–07, saw him sparkle and attracted offers in the January transfer window of between £5 million and £10 million for a player who was as yet only an Under-21 international. West Ham offered £10 million, but Ashley accepted the Villa in a deal which was worth £8 million rising to £9.75 million with add ons.

He settled in quickly at Villa Park and was called up to the England squad on 31 August 2007 by Steve McLaren. He did not play in this game, nor in two later games, but he finally made his international debut at half-time in a friendly against Austria on 16 November 2007, replacing Joe Cole. Caps against Switzerland and Trinidad in friendlies in February and June 2008 followed, with a fourth in a friendly against Germany in November 2008.

These caps reflected the enormous impression Ashley had made on the Premiership in his first full season, 2007–08. He finished second to Cesc Fabregas in assists with 17, and was included in the Premier League Team of the Year – along with David James as one of only two players not from the Big Four of Liverpool, Manchester United, Arsenal and Chelsea. He won the Player of the Month award in April and October 2008, joining a select band who have won it more than once, including Christiano Renaldo, Wayne Rooney and Steven Gerrard. On 4 November 2008 he signed a new enhanced four-year contract. He then won a third Player of the Month award for December, becoming the first player to win three in one calendar year. He was, not surprisingly, Professional Footballer Association Young Player of the Year in 2008–09.

He was established in the Villa squad as a regular, but not at England level. His second, third and fourth caps show that new manager Fabio Capello to begin with saw him as a super sub, coming on late in the game gainst tiring defenders with his pace and accurate crossing. His fifth cap against Andorra saw him replace Gerrard for the whole of the second half, while his sixth cap against Holland saw him start but be replaced by Milner in the 68th minute as England chased the game. Milner then became a regular, Ashley still a back number who was not taken to the World Cup despite his seven caps – with only one start. He needed to up his game, and he did.

Ashley Young played initially as a winger, operating on both sides of the field. He is known for his pace, passing ability and shooting skills. His crosses are particularly feared by the opposition, as he whips the ball into the penalty area with pace and accuracy. However, in the 2010–11 season he began to play as a withdrawn inside-forward, operating behind a lone striker, proving to have a superb football brain, putting through accurate passes behind the opposition defence, making him even more valuable to the team. He completed 150 appearances for Villa on 9 May 2010 in the home match against Blackburn, making 147 starts

another pacy midfield/winger player who might score against a tiring defence. He had already replaced Walcott after 46 minutes of the Hungary game on 11 August 2010, Defoe after 87 minutes of the Bulgaria game on 3 September 2010, and would replace Barry after 46 minutes of the loss against France on 17 November 2010. However, while he was again used as a super sub against Denmark on 9 February 2011, after 46 minutes when he replaced Rooney, he scored the winning goal.

After scoring this first England goal, in a side which ended with three Villa players on the pitch, he said he wanted to form a partnership with Darren Bent, commenting 'if you play together at club level then you know each other's movements for the international stage. Playing through the middle gives you a chance to score more goals'. Clearly he sees himself as a striker not a winger – and with Darren Bent if all goes to plan. He is developing at England level as a predator in the Defoe mould, and has every chance of staking a real claim at England level.

and three substitute appearances. By the end of the 2009–10 season he had scored 29 goals, nine coming in the 2009–10 season. He was, however, developing his striking role rather than remaining mainly a provider.

With England rebuilding after the disappointment of the 2010 World Cup campaign, Ashley has a chance to force his way into the England reckoning, which he shows the ability to do. Of the five games he played up to and including 9 February 2011, he only started one – the 0–0 draw against the minnows of Montenegro, where he was substituted by Sean Wright Phillips after 74 minutes –

Bibliography

Aston Villa

Aston Villa The history of a great football club, 1874–1961, Peter Morris, The Sportsman's book club, London 1962,

Aston Villa 1874ñ1998, Graham McColl, Hamlyn Illustrated History, 1998

Aston Villa Greats Leon Hickman, Sportsprint Publishing, 1990

The Aston Villa Story, Ian Johnson, Arthur Baker Ltd, London 1981

Aston Villa The Complete Record, Rob Bishop, Frank Holt, DB Books 2010

Billy Walker; once, twice, three times a winner, Edward Giles, Desert Island Books 2008

The Complete Encyclopaedia of Aston Villa Tony Matthews, Britespot 2001. (TM 01)

David Platt; Achieving The Goal: An autobiography, Richard Cohen Books 1995

Football in the Blood (autobiography), Billy Walker, Stanley Paul 1960

Forever Villa David Instone Thomas Publications 2005

The Gerry Hitchens Story: From Mine to Milan, Simon Goodyear, Breedon Books, 2009

Hero and Villain Paul Merson with Ian Ridley, Collins Willow 2000

The Legends of Aston Villa, Tony Matthews, Breedon Books 2007

McMullan To O'Leary Claret and Blue Managers, Dave Woodhall, Heroes Publishing, 2003

Pinnacle of the Perry Barr Pets, Simon Page Juma 1987

Prophet or Traitor? The Jimmy Hogan Story, Norman Fox, Parrs Wood Press 2003

The Road to Rotterdam Rob Bishop, Britespot October 2001

Who's Who of Aston Villa Tony Matthews Mainstream Publishing 2004 (TM 04)

The Villains Day to Day Life at Villa Park, Simon Betts, Mainstream Publishing 1998

Football history

Association Football And The Men Who Made It Alfred Gibson & William Pickford. Vols I–IV, Caxton Publishing Company, 1906 (Gibson & Pickford)

The Book of Football A Complete History and Record of the Association and Rugby Games, The Amalgamated Press, London 1906

Corinthians And Cricketers Edward Grayson (G.O. Smith) Yore Publications 1966

England 1872–1940, International Federation of Football History and Statistics (no publisher, no date, in FA Library) (used as IFFHS)

The Father of Modern Sport The Life and Times of Charles Alcock. Keith Booth, Parrs Wood Press, Manchester 2002

Football League Tables 1888–2005, Ed Michael Robinson, Soccer Books Ltd, 2005

Football The Golden Age, John Tennant, Cassell 2001

100 Seasons of League Football 1888–1988, Bryon Butler, Queen Anne Press, 1987, revised edition 1998

History of England

Don't Shoot the Manager; The revealing story of England's soccer bosses, Jimmy Greaves with Norman Giller, Boxtree 1993

England Expects A History of the England Football Team, James Corbett, Aurum 2006

Farewell But Not Goodbye: My Autobiography Bobby Robson. Little information on Villa players, even David Platt who he brought into the England team.

Internationalists Who's Who, Douglas Lammy, 1990

FA Yearbook 2008–09

FA Yearbook 2009–10

FA Yearbook 2010–11

The FA Complete Guide to England Players Since 1945 Stanley Paul 1993, up to June 1993

Websites

England; International Results 1872–2007 http://www.rsssf.com/tablese/engñintres1872.html. prepared and maintained for the Rec.Sports.Soccer Statistics Foundation. By Barrie Courtney BzCourtney@aol.com.

England Football Online; http://www.englandfootballonline.com/CmpBC /CmpBCTmHist.html.

ND - #0300 - 270225 - C0 - 234/156/12 - PB - 9781780913780 - Gloss Lamination